Quilted Comforts
for the
Home

LEISURE ARTS, INC.
Little Rock, Arkansas

EDITORIAL STAFF

Vice President and Editor-in-Chief: Sandra Graham Case
Executive Director of Publications: Cheryl Nodine Gunnells
Senior Director of Publications: Susan White Sullivan
Director of Designer Relations: Debra Nettles
Licensed Product Coordinator: Lisa Truxton Curton
Publications Director: Kristine Anderson Mertes
Editorial Director: Susan Frantz Wiles
Photography Director: Stephen Wilson
Senior Art Operations Director: Jeff Curtis

TECHNICAL
Managing Editor: Cheryl R. Johnson
Technical Writers: Frances Huddleston, Lisa Lancaster, and Jean W. Lewis

EDITORIAL
Associate Editors: Susan McManus Johnson and Kimberly L. Ross

DESIGN
Designer: Linda Diehl Tiano
Technical Assistants: Brenda Bullock and Karla Edgar

ART

Art Publications Director: Rhonda Shelby
Art Imaging Director: Mark Hawkins
Art Category Manager: Lora Puls
Graphic Artists: Dayle Cosh, Dana Vaughn, and Elaine Wheat
Photography Stylist: Janna Laughlin
Staff Photographer: Russell Ganser
Publishing Systems Administrator: Becky Riddle
Publishing Systems Assistants: Clint Hanson, Myra S. Means, and Chris Wertenberger

BUSINESS STAFF

Publisher: Rick Barton
Vice President, Finance: Tom Siebenmorgen
Director of Corporate Planning and Development: Laticia Mull Dittrich
Vice President, Retail Marketing: Bob Humphrey
Vice President, Sales: Ray Shelgosh
Vice President, National Accounts: Pam Stebbins
Director of Sales and Services: Margaret Reinold
Vice President, Operations: Jim Dittrich
Comptroller, Operations: Rob Thieme
Retail Customer Service Managers: Sharon Hall and Stan Raynor
Print Production Manager: Fred F. Pruss

We have made every effort to ensure that these instructions are accurate and complete. We cannot, however, be responsible for human error, typographical mistakes, or variations in individual work.
Made in the United States of America.

Softcover ISBN 1-57486-317-7

10 9 8 7 6 5 4 3 2 1

Table of Contents

Cottage Comfort

As Mary Engelbreit likes to say, "Home is where the heart is." You can make your home a haven with these cottage-cozy accents to quilt or craft. Start by creating the Cottage Comfort Quilt in shades of red, antique white, and soft blue. The blocks are an old-fashioned design that has warmed hearts and protected against winter's chill for well over a century. To see more of these cozy home accents, just turn the page.

"Ah! There is nothing like staying at home, for real comfort." —Jane Austen

Each of these cottage-inspired floral designs will bring your home a little closer to being a slice of heaven. Treat yourself to a Moments in Time Wall Hanging (opposite), a wise work of appliqué, embroidery, and simple sewing. Or get organized with a Keepsake Box (opposite) topped in dimensional flowers created with fabric. Pins and needles needn't be prickly matters — keep them in a Teacup Pincushion (opposite). And have you noticed the most terrific thing about pillows — you can never have too many! Stitch a flower-cornered Cottage Comfort Pillow (right), or button up a Strip-Bordered Pillow (below) with easy piecing and pretty appliqué.

COTTAGE COMFORT QUILT

QUILT SIZE: 80" x 80" (203 cm x 203 cm)
BLOCK SIZE: 8" x 8" (20 cm x 20 cm)

FABRIC REQUIREMENTS

Yardage is based on 45"w fabric.

$2^3/_8$ yds (2.1 m) of red solid
$^1/_8$ yd (11 cm) each of 25 assorted light prints
$3^3/_4$ yds (3.4 m) of blue print
$8^1/_8$ yds (7.4 m) for backing
1 yd (91 cm) for binding

You will also need:

Queen size batting

CUTTING OUT THE PIECES

All measurements include a $^1/_4$" seam allowance.

FOR EACH PIECED BLOCK

1. From red solid:
    *   Cut 3 squares $2^7/_8$" x $2^7/_8$". Cut squares once diagonally to make 6 small triangles.
    *   Cut 1 square $4^7/_8$" x $4^7/_8$". Cut square once diagonally to make 2 large triangles.
2. From each light print:
    *   Cut 5 squares $2^7/_8$" x $2^7/_8$". Cut each square in half once diagonally to make 10 small triangles.
    *   Cut 4 squares $2^1/_2$" x $2^1/_2$".

SETTING SQUARES, SETTING TRIANGLES, AND BORDERS

1. From red print:
    *   Cut 2 lengthwise top and bottom third border strips 2" x $74^1/_2$".
    *   Cut 2 lengthwise side third border strips 2" x $77^1/_2$".
    *   Cut 132 strips $1^1/_2$" x 3" for pieced border.
    *   Cut 4 strips $1^1/_2$" x 4" for pieced border corners.
2. From blue print:
    *   Cut 16 squares $8^1/_2$" x $8^1/_2$" for setting squares.
    *   Cut 4 squares $12^5/_8$" x $12^5/_8$". Cut each square twice diagonally to make 16 setting triangles.
    *   Cut 2 squares $6^5/_8$" x $6^5/_8$". Cut each square once diagonally to make 4 corner setting triangles.
    *   Cut 2 lengthwise top/bottom second border strips 4" x $67^1/_2$".
    *   Cut 2 lengthwise side second border strips 4" x $74^1/_2$".
    *   Cut 2 lengthwise top/bottom fourth border strips $3^1/_2$" x $77^1/_2$".
    *   Cut 2 lengthwise side fourth border strips $3^1/_2$" x $83^1/_2$".

*   Cut 66 squares $3^3/_8$" x $3^3/_8$". Cut each square once diagonally to make 132 triangles for pieced border.
*   Cut 2 squares $2^3/_8$" x $2^3/_8$". Cut each square once diagonally to make 4 triangles for pieced border corners.

MAKING THE QUILT TOP

Follow Piecing and Pressing, page 85, to make quilt top.

PIECED BLOCK

1. Sew together 1 small red and 1 small light triangle to make a triangle square (Fig.1). Repeat to make a total of 6 triangle-squares.

Fig. 1

2. Sew 1 small light triangle to 2 sides of 2 triangle-squares (Fig.2).

Fig. 2

3. Refer to Block Diagram to sew together triangles, triangle-squares, and squares to make block.

Block Diagram (make 25)

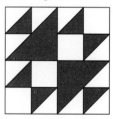

4. Referring to Assembly Diagram, sew pieced blocks, setting squares, setting triangles, and corner setting triangles into diagonal rows. Sew rows together to make center section of quilt top.

PIECED BORDER

1. Referring to Fig. 3, sew 1 short red strip to 1 short side of each blue border triangle. Make 64 Unit 1's and 68 Unit 2's.

Fig. 3

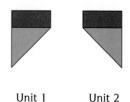

Unit 1   Unit 2

2. With Unit 2 on top, sew Unit 2 to Unit 1, beginning at dot and reinforcing stitching. (Fig. 4).

Fig. 4

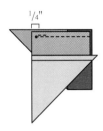

3. With Unit 1 on top, fold back point and finger press (Fig. 5). Being careful not to catch folded edge of Unit 1 in seam, sew another Unit 1 to Unit 2, ending and reinforcing at dot (Fig. 6).

Fig. 5

Fig. 6

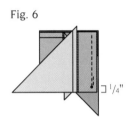

4. Unfold point and complete seam (Fig. 7).

Fig. 7

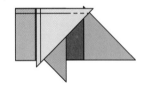

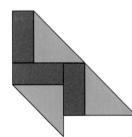

5. Repeat Steps 2-4 to complete one pieced border with a total of 17 Unit 1's and 16 Unit 2's.
6. Repeat Steps 1-5 to make 4 pieced borders.
7. Sew 1 red corner strip to the Unit 1 end of each border.
8. Referring to Assembly Diagram for orientation and starting and stopping 1/4" from each corner, sew borders to center section of quilt top.

9. To miter corners, fold 1 corner of quilt top diagonally with right sides together and matching raw edges of border. Pin in place, then reinforcing stitching, sew diagonally from corner of border to corner of quilt. (Fig. 8)

Fig. 8

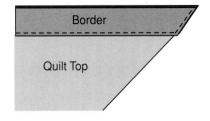

10. Sew 1 blue border corner to each corner of quilt top.
11. Follow **Adding Squared Borders**, page 88, to sew top/bottom second borders, then side borders to quilt top. Repeat for third and fourth borders.

COMPLETING THE QUILT

1. Follow **Quilting**, page 88, to mark layer, and quilt. Our quilt is hand quilted with a grid pattern in the center, cross-hatching in the pieced border, and a triple cable in the outer borders.
2. Cut a 31" square of binding fabric. Follow **Binding**, page 91, to bind quilt using 2¹/₂"w bias binding with mitered corners.

Assembly Diagram

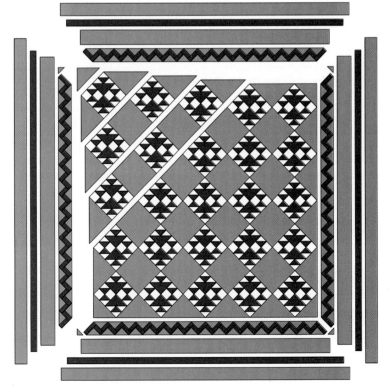

MOMENTS IN TIME WALL HANGING

SIZE: 22$\frac{1}{2}$" x 21$\frac{1}{2}$" (58 cm x 55 cm)

FABRIC REQUIREMENTS

Yardage is based on 45"w fabric.

$\frac{5}{8}$ yd (57 cm) of white solid
$\frac{1}{4}$ yd (23 cm) of blue print for border and binding
$\frac{1}{4}$ yd (23 cm) of small red check
$\frac{3}{4}$ yd (69 cm) of fabric for backing
Assorted print scraps for appliqués

You will also need:

Tracing paper
Embroidery floss: dark grey, yellow, light green, dark green, red, blue, and to match appliqués
2$\frac{1}{4}$ yds (2.1 m) of $\frac{1}{2}$"w cream crochet trim
Fine-point water-soluble fabric marking pen
Paper-backed fusible web

CUTTING OUT THE PIECES

All measurements include a $\frac{1}{4}$" seam allowance.

1. **From white solid:**
    *   Cut 1 rectangle 17$\frac{1}{2}$" x 18$\frac{1}{2}$".
2. **From blue print:**
    *   Cut 2 side borders 1$\frac{1}{2}$" x 15$\frac{1}{2}$".
    *   Cut 2 top/bottom borders 1$\frac{1}{2}$" x 18$\frac{1}{2}$".
3. **From small red check:**
    *   Cut 2 side borders 2$\frac{1}{2}$" x 17$\frac{1}{2}$" ".
    *   Cut 2 top/bottom borders 2$\frac{1}{2}$" x 22$\frac{1}{2}$".

MAKING THE WALL HANGING

*Follow **Embroidery Stitches**, page 93, for all embroidery.*
*Follow **Piecing and Pressing**, page 85, to add borders after completing appliqué and embroidery designs.*

1. Centering white solid rectangle over pattern, pages 14 - 15, use water-soluble pen to trace pattern, moving fabric as needed to trace each half.
2. Use a pencil to trace each appliqué pattern onto tracing paper; cut out patterns. Follow manufacturer's instructions to fuse web to wrong side of appliqué fabric. Draw around pattern on right side of appliqué fabrics adding a small underlap to the edges which are covered by another piece; cut out appliqués. Fuse appliqués to white rectangle. Refer to photo, page 6, and use marker to draw a vine with Lazy Daisy leaves around design.

3. Using 2 strands of matching floss, Blanket Stitch around edges of all appliqués.
4. Using 3 strands of green floss, Stem Stitch each vine and add Lazy Daisy leaves along each vine.
5. Using 3 strands of dark grey floss, Running Stitch remaining letters.
6. Using 3 strands of red, blue, or green floss, add Lazy Daisy flowers. Using 3 strands of yellow floss, add a French Knot center to each flower.
7. Trim appliquéd and embroidered rectangle to 15$\frac{1}{2}$" x 16$\frac{1}{2}$".
8. Sew 1 blue print side border to each side of rectangle. Sew blue print top and bottom borders to rectangle.
9. Sew 1 red check side border to each side of rectangle. Sew red check top and bottom borders to rectangle.

COMPLETING THE WALL HANGING

1. Follow **Quilting**, page 88, to layer, and quilt. Our quilt is machine quilted "in the ditch" around the center rectangle and along each border seam.
2. Follow **Binding**, page 91, to bind quilt using 1$\frac{1}{2}$"w straight grain double-fold binding with mitered corners.
3. Placing edge of lace trim along seam between borders, stitch lace to wall hanging.

COTTAGE COMFORT PILLOW

SIZE: 11$\frac{1}{2}$" x 11$\frac{1}{2}$" (29 cm x 29 cm)

FABRIC REQUIREMENTS

Yardage is based on 45"w fabric.

$\frac{1}{4}$ yd (23 cm) of light blue floral print
$\frac{3}{8}$ yd (34 cm) of blue floral print
$\frac{3}{8}$ yd (34 cm) of red check
12" x 12" (30 cm x 30 cm) square of muslin
Scraps of dark pink, green and yellow prints
12" x 12" (30 cm x 30 cm) square of batting

You will also need:

Paper-backed fusible web
Embroidery floss: Dark pink, green, and yellow
Polyester fiberfill
1$\frac{1}{2}$ yds of $\frac{1}{4}$" (7mm) diameter cord

CUTTING OUT THE PIECES

All measurements include a $\frac{1}{4}$" seam allowance.

1. **From light blue floral print:**
   - Cut 2 squares 6$\frac{5}{8}$" x 6$\frac{5}{8}$". Cut each square in half once diagonally to make 4 triangles.
2. **From blue floral print:**
   - For pillow back, cut 1 square 12" x 12".
   - Cut 5 squares 2$\frac{7}{8}$" x 2$\frac{7}{8}$". Cut each square in half once diagonally to make 10 small triangles.
   - Cut 4 squares 2$\frac{1}{2}$" x 2$\frac{1}{2}$".
3. **From red check:**
   - Cut 3 squares 2$\frac{7}{8}$" x 2$\frac{7}{8}$". Cut each square in half once diagonally to make 6 small triangles.
   - Cut 1 square 4$\frac{7}{8}$" x 4$\frac{7}{8}$". Cut square in half once diagonally to make 2 medium triangles.
   - For welting, cut 1 bias strip 2" x 50", piecing as necessary.

MAKING THE PILLOW

*Follow **Piecing and Pressing**, page 85, to make pillow top.*

1. Sew together 1 small red and 1 small blue triangle to make a triangle square (Fig.1). Repeat to make a total of 6 triangle-squares.

Fig. 1

2. Sew 1 small blue triangle to 2 sides of 2 triangle-squares (Fig.2).

Fig. 2

3. Refer to **Pillow Top Diagram** to sew together triangles and squares.

Pillow Top Diagram

4. Refer to **Preparing Fusible Appliqués**, page 87, to use flower, flower center, and leaf patterns, page 15, to prepare and fuse appliqués to pillow top. Follow **Embroidery Stitches**, page 93, to Blanket Stitch around appliqués using matching floss.
5. Refer to **Quilting**, page 88, to layer muslin, batting, and pillow top and to outline quilt around the flowers and blue triangles. Trim batting and backing even with pillow top.
6. Refer to **Pillow Finishing**, page 95, to add welting to pillow top and to finish pillow.

STRIP-BORDERED PILLOW

SIZE: 9¹/₂" x 19" (24 cm x 48 cm)

FABRIC REQUIREMENTS

Yardage is based on 45"w fabric.

³/₈ yd (34 cm) of cream solid
³/₈ yd (34 cm) of light blue floral print
¹/₈ yd (11 cm) of red check
Scraps of dark pink, green, light blue, medium blue and yellow prints

You will also need:

Tracing paper
Paper-backed fusible web
Embroidery floss: dark pink, green, blue and yellow
1 yd (91 cm) of ¹/₂"w cream crochet trim
Polyester fiberfill
6 cream ³/₄" (19 mm) buttons

CUTTING OUT THE PIECES

All measurements include a ¹/₄" seam allowance.

1. From cream solid:
   • Cut 1 rectangle 9¹/₂" x 12¹/₂".
   • Cut 2 rectangles 10" x 13 " for inner pillow.
2. From red check:
   • Cut 2 top/bottom borders 1³/₄" x 10¹/₂".
   • Cut 2 side borders 1³/₄" x 10".
3. From light blue floral print:
   • Cut 1 rectangle 10" x 27¹/₂" for pillow back.
   • Cut 2 rectangles 4" x 10" for front facings.
4. From assorted scraps:
   • Cut strips 4" long by random widths which, when sewn together, total 10" high.

MAKING THE PILLOW

Follow Embroidery Stitches, page 93 for all embroidery.
Follow Piecing and Pressing, page 85, to add borders after completing appliqué and embroidery designs.

1. Use a pencil to trace appliqué patterns, page 14, onto tracing paper; cut out patterns. Follow manufacturer's instructions to fuse web to wrong side of appliqué fabrics. Draw around patterns on right side of appliqué fabrics; cut out appliqués. Referring to photo, page 5, arrange, then fuse appliqués to cream rectangle. Use pencil to lightly draw vine at each end of appliqué.
2. Using 2 strands of matching floss, Blanket Stitch around edges of all appliqués. Using 3 strands of green floss, Stem Stitch each vine.
3. Trim appliquéd rectangle to 7¹/₂" x 10¹/₂".
4. Sew red check top/bottom borders to rectangle. Sew each side border to rectangle.

5. Placing edge of lace trim along seam allowance between border and appliquéd rectangle, stitch lace to pillow front.
6. For pieced borders, sew 4" long strips together to form 2 side borders 4" x 10. Sew 1 border to each end of pillow front. Sew 1 facing to each end of pillow front.
7. With right sides together, sew pillow front and back together along long edges. Press short raw edges ¹/₄" to wrong side. Fold facing back along seam allowance and hand stitch in place.
8. With right sides together and leaving an opening for turning, sew inner pillow rectangles together. Turn to right side, stuff with fiberfill, then sew opening closed.
9. Insert inner pillow into one open end of pillow. Sewing through all layers, sew 3 buttons to each end of pillow.

TEACUP PINCUSHION

MATERIALS NEEDED

1 white demitasse cup and saucer
8" circle of red check fabric
Thread
Polyester fiberfill
Hot glue
Assorted small stickers

MAKING THE PINCUSHION

1. To make pincushion, turn edge of circle ¹/₄" to wrong side and make a Running Stitch around edge using 2 strands of thread. Place a fist-size ball of fiberfill in center of circle. Pull threads from both ends, adding fiberfill as needed to make a firm ball which will fit into cup. Tie thread ends into a knot; clip threads.
2. Place pincushion in cup. If desired, hot glue in place.
3. Cutting apart as necessary, adhere stickers to cup and saucer.

KEEPSAKE BOX

FABRIC REQUIREMENTS

Yardage is based on 45"w fabric.

$1/8$ yd (11 cm) of small red check
$1/4$ yd (23 cm) of light blue print
$1/8$ yd (11 cm) of medium blue print
Assorted scraps of blue check, dark pink, red, green and light green prints

You will also need:

Oval cardboard box with lid (ours measures 9" long x 7" wide x 4" high)
Lightweight fusible fleece
Spray adhesive
$1/2$"w cream crochet trim
Craft glue
Paper-backed fusible web
16 assorted yellow buttons
1 blue $5/8$" diameter (16 mm) button
12 red $1/2$" diameter (13 mm) buttons
Yellow embroidery floss
1 wooden thread spool
Scraps of polyester fiberfill

MAKING THE KEEPSAKE BOX

1. To cover box lid, trace around lid on wrong side of fusible fleece. Cut out fleece on drawn line then fuse to lid.

2. Trace around lid on wrong side of light blue print. Cut out fabric $1/2$" outside drawn line. Use spray adhesive to adhere fabric to lid. Measure the height and circumference of box lid; add $1/2$" to each measurement. Cut a piece of medium blue print this measurement. Press raw edges under $1/4$" to wrong side. Beginning and ending at center back, glue fabric strip around lid edge.

3. Cut 2 pieces of crochet trim the circumference of the lid plus $1/2$". Turning under one raw edge and beginning at center back with raw edge, use craft glue to adhere trim to top and bottom edges of box lid.

4. To cover box bottom, measure the height and circumference of bottom. Add $1/2$" to each measurement. Cut a piece of red check this measurement. Press under one short raw edge $1/4$". Beginning and ending at center back, center fabric strip on box side. Pressing top raw edge to inside and bottom raw edge under box, glue strip to side of box.

5. To make padded flowers and leaves, layer fabric scrap with wrong side up, fusible web with paper removed, fusible fleece with adhesive side up, and fabric scrap with right side up. Fuse all layers. Use patterns, below, to cut 5 round flowers, 2 scalloped flowers, 6 rounded leaves and 4 pointed leaves. From red check fabric, cut 2 flower centers then fuse centers to scalloped flowers. Use yellow floss to sew buttons to flower centers.

6. Center, then glue spool to box lid. Using a long needle, sew blue button to top of spool, anchoring floss through box lid. Refer to photo to arrange, then glue flowers, leaves and buttons to lid, using small pieces of fiberfill under flowers and leaves to add height to selected flowers.

7. Use yellow floss to make an X through the holes in red buttons. Bringing thread ends to back, tie ends into a knot; clips ends close to knot. Spacing evenly, glue buttons around center of box.

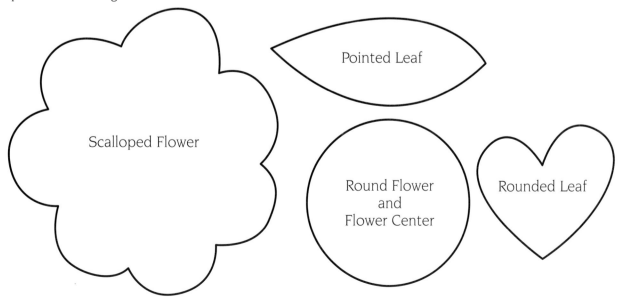

Scalloped Flower

Pointed Leaf

Round Flower and Flower Center

Rounded Leaf

Round Flower
Center

Top
Leaf

Heart

Right
Leaf

Bottom
Leaf

Left Leaf

Scalloped Flower
Center

Scalloped Flower
Highlight

Scalloped Flower

Round Flower

TIME

MEAS

CLOCKS

MOM

14

Mary's Flower Garden

Joseph Joubert once wrote, "All gardeners live in beautiful places because they make them so." You can make your favorite room as lovely as any outdoor retreat by re-creating Mary's Flower Garden. This spring-fresh appliquéd quilt is just the beginning — turn the page to see more of Mary's delightful garden designs.

Anytime you look at this Ruffles & Blossoms Pillow (above), you'll see all the joyful colors of springtime. And the creative secret behind the sweet Chenille Valance (opposite, above) may surprise you. Make the quick Flower-Shaped Pillow (opposite, below), and you're ready to reap the beautiful benefits of a year-'round indoor garden.

"Oh, who can tell the range
of joy or set the bounds
of beauty?" —Sara Teasdale

Have you guessed the secret to the fluffy flowers on this Chenille Wall Hanging? Along with the bouquet on the Chenille Valance (page 19), these soft creations are easily made from ordinary cotton fabric!

FLOWER GARDEN QUILT

TWIN QUILT SIZE: 68" x 88" (173 cm x 224 cm)

FABRIC REQUIREMENTS

Yardage is based on 45"w fabric.

$2^1/4$ yds (2.1 m) of white solid
$2^1/4$ yds (2.1 m) of black and white stripe
$2^1/4$ yd (2.1 m) of yellow floral print
$2^1/4$ yd (2.1 m) of yellow small print
$5^3/8$ yds (4.9 m) of fabric for backing
$1/2$ yd (46 cm) of fabric for binding
$1^1/4$ yds (1.1 m) of fabric for stems
Assorted prints for appliqués

You will also need:

$14^1/4$ yds (13 m) of yellow jumbo rickrack
6 yds (5.5 m) of $1/2$"w (13 mm) fusible web tape
72" x 90" (183 cm x 229 cm) of batting
Transparent monofilament thread

CUTTING OUT THE PIECES

All measurements include a $1/4$" seam allowance unless otherwise noted.

1. From white solid:
   - Cut 3 rectangles $12^1/2$" x $70^1/2$".
2. From black and white stripe:
   - Cut 4 sashing strips $1^1/2$" x $68^1/2$".
   - Cut 2 sashing strips 2" x $68^1/2$".
   - Cut 2 sashing strips 2" x $51^1/2$".
3. From yellow floral print:
   - Cut 2 rectangles $7^1/2$" x $68^1/2$".
4. From yellow small print:
   - Cut 2 side borders $8^1/2$" x $71^1/2$".
   - Cut 2 top/bottom borders $8^1/2$" x $67^1/2$".
5. From fabric for stems:
   - Cut 4 bias strips 1" x 45".

PIECING THE QUILT TOP

1. For stems, press each long edge of bias strips $1/4$" to wrong side. Centering tape, fuse web tape to wrong side of folded bias strips.

2. (Note: White rectangles will be trimmed after they are appliquéd. Remember to fuse the appliqués within a 10" x 68" design area.) Referring to **Preparing Fusible Appliqués**, page 87, and **Quilt Top Diagram**, page 22, use patterns for flowers 1-3, flower centers 1-3, and leaves 1-3, pages 25-27, to prepare and fuse appliqués and bias stems (trimmed to lengths as needed) to white solid rectangles. Refer to **Invisible Appliqué**, page 88, to stitch appliqués and stems in place.

3. Centering design in panel, trim each panel to $10^1/2$" x $68^1/2$".

4. Matching right side of rickrack to right side of fabric, center rickrack along seam allowance and baste along long edge of each yellow floral print rectangle.

5. Designate 1 end of each panel as top. Place appliquéd rectangles side-by-side on flat surface. On left panel, sew a 2"w striped sashing strip to left side of panel and a $1^1/2$"w striped sashing strip to right side of panel.

6. On center panel, sew a $1^1/2$"w striped sashing strip to each long side of panel.

7. On right panel, sew a $1^1/2$"w striped sashing strip to left side of panel and a 2"w striped sashing strip to right side of panel.

8. Matching right sides and raw edges and with rickrack sandwiched in between, refer to **Quilt Top Diagram** to sew appliquéd rectangles and yellow floral print rectangles together. Press rickrack towards sashing strips.

9. Sew remaining striped sashing strips to top and bottom of quilt top.

10. Matching right side of rickrack to right side of fabric, center rickrack along seam allowance and baste along each edge of quilt top.

11. Sew 1 side border to each side of quilt top. Press rickrack toward sashing. Sew top/bottom borders to quilt top. Press rickrack toward sashing.

COMPLETING THE QUILT

1. Follow **Quilting**, page 88, to mark layer, and quilt as desired. Our quilt is machine quilted in-the-ditch around the black/white sashing. In the borders we quilted a repeat leaf pattern with tulips in the corners. The yellow floral panels are quilted with ripples and there are tendrils in the white panels around the flowers.
2. Follow **Binding**, page 91, to bind quilt using 9^1/$_2$ yards of 1^1/$_2$"w single-fold binding with mitered corners.

Quilt Top Diagram

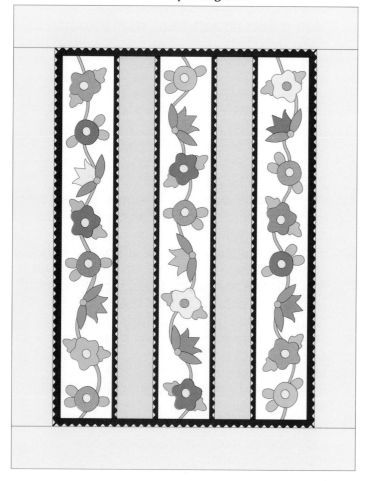

RUFFLES & BLOSSOMS PILLOW
SIZE: 14" x 14" (36 cm x 36 cm)

FABRIC REQUIREMENTS
Yardage is based on 45"w fabric.
^{3}/$_8$ yd (34 cm) of white solid
^{3}/$_4$ yd (69 cm) of yellow print
^{5}/$_8$ yd (57 cm) of green check
Assorted prints for appliqués
You will also need:
14" (36 cm) square pillow form
4 pink ^{7}/$_8$" (22 mm) diameter buttons
Transparent monofilament thread

CUTTING OUT THE PIECES
All measurements include a ^{1}/$_4$" seam allowance.
1. **From white solid:**
   - For pillow front, cut 1 square 10^1/$_2$" x 10^1/$_2$".
2. **From yellow print:**
   - For borders, cut 2 strips 2^1/$_2$" x 10^1/$_2$".
   - For borders, cut 2 strips 2^1/$_2$" x 14^1/$_2$".
   - For backing, cut 1 square 14^1/$_2$" x 14^1/$_2$".
3. **From green check:**
   - For ruffle, cut a 6" x 112" strip (pieced as necessary).

MAKING THE PILLOW
1. For pillow top, sew short yellow print borders to two opposite sides of white solid square. Sew long yellow print borders to remaining sides of white solid square.
2. Refer to **Preparing Fusible Appliqués**, page 87, and use patterns for flowers 2-4, flower centers 2-4, and leaves 2-4, pages 25, 26 and 28 to prepare and fuse appliqués to pillow top. Refer to **Invisible Appliqué**, page 88, to stitch appliqués in place.
3. Refer to **Pillow Finishing**, page 95, to add ruffle to pillow top and to finish pillow.
4. Sew 1 button to each corner of pillow.

CHENILLE VALANCE

Fits window approximately 45" (114 cm) wide or less.

FABRIC REQUIREMENTS

Yardage is based on 45"w fabric.

- 1/2 yd (46 cm) of pink chenille fabric
- 1/2 yd (46 cm) of yellow chenille fabric
- 1/8 yd (11 cm) of green chenille fabric
- 3/8 yd (34 cm) of multi-color chenille fabric
- 1/2 yd (46 cm) of cream cotton fabric
- 1/2 yd (46 cm) of yellow cotton fabric
- 1/2 yd (46 cm) of green cotton fabric

You will also need:

- 2 yds (1.8 m) of 1" (25 mm) diameter cream pom-pom fringe
- 3 pink 7/8" (22 mm) diameter buttons
- Stiff bristle brush

CUTTING OUT THE PIECES

All measurements include a 1/2" seam allowance unless otherwise noted.

1. From pink chenille fabric:
   - Cut 2 side panels 14" x 15"
2. From yellow chenille fabric:
   - Cut 2 panels 13 1/2" x 15".
3. From green chenille fabric:
   - Cut 2 sashing strips 15" x 2 1/2".
4. From multi-color chenille fabric:
   - Cut 1 rod pocket 67 1/2" x 6" (pieced as necessary).
5. From cream cotton fabric:
   - Cut fabric panel 15 1/2" x 17".
6. From yellow cotton fabric:
   - Cutting on the bias grain of the fabric, cut 4 rectangles 6" x 12".
7. From green cotton fabric:
   - Cutting on the bias grain of the fabric, cut 4 rectangles 6" x 12".

MAKING THE VALANCE

1. To make chenille flower appliqué, draw lines parallel to the long edges 1/2" apart on the right side of 1 yellow cotton fabric rectangle. With right sides up, stack all yellow cotton fabric rectangles. Alternating sewing direction, stitch along all drawn lines. Cutting halfway between each stitching line, cut strips apart.
2. Repeat Step 1 for green cotton fabric.
3. Place cream cotton fabric over pattern, page 29. Trace pattern onto fabric panel.
4. To stitch flower appliqué, match stitching line on 1 yellow cotton fabric strip to drawn line on panel. Sew strip to fabric panel, backstitching at beginning and end of each strip. To add another strip, stop stitching 1/4" from end, place new strip under the end; backstitch, and then continue stitching. When stitching a curve, stitch slowly, stopping with needle down; raise presser foot to adjust strip to avoid pleats or puckers.
5. To stitch stem and leaves, repeat Step 4 for green cotton fabric.
6. To fluff chenille, use a spray bottle to wet fabric strips and brush with a stiff-bristle brush.
7. Trim cream cotton panel to 13 1/2" x 15".
8. Sew 1 button to center of each flower.
9. Sew green chenille fabric sashing strips to each side of cream cotton fabric panel.
10. Sew yellow chenille fabric panel to each side of green sashing strip.
11. Sew pink chenille fabric panel to each side of yellow chenille fabric panel.
12. Sew rod pocket to top of pieced valance.
13. To hem side edges, turn fabric 1/2" to wrong side; turn 1/2" to wrong side again. Topstitch hem in place.
14. Press long raw edge of rod pocket 1/2" to wrong side. Fold strip in half with folded edge covering seam allowance. Topstitch along lower folded edge. Topstitch again 1 3/4" from previous stitching to form rod pocket.
15. To hem, turn lower edge of valance 1/2" to wrong side; turn 1/2" to wrong side again. Baste folded edge in place. Place seam allowance of pom-pom fringe on wrong side of folded hem; topstitch in place through all thicknesses.

Valance Diagram

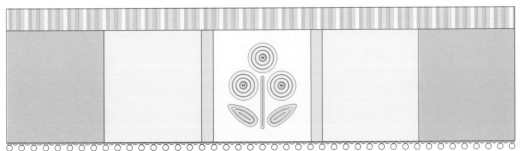

CHENILLE WALL HANGING

SIZE: 24" x 24" (60 x 60 cm)

FABRIC REQUIREMENTS

Yardage is based on 45"w fabric.

$1/4$ yd (23 cm) each of cream, yellow, pink, blue, and green chenille fabrics

$1/2$ yd (46 cm) of multi-color chenille fabric

$1^5/8$ yds (1.5 m) of cream cotton fabric

$1/2$ yd (46 cm) of yellow cotton fabric

$1/2$ yd (46 cm) of green cotton fabric

You will also need:

3 yds (2.7 m) of 1" (25 mm) diameter cream pom-pom fringe

25" x 25" (64 cm x 64 cm) square of polyester bonded batting

3 pink $7/8$" (22 mm) diameter buttons

Stiff bristle brush

CUTTING OUT THE PIECES

All measurements include a $1/4$" seam allowance unless otherwise noted.

1. From each of cream, yellow, pink, blue, and green chenille fabrics:
   - Cut 1 5" strip. Randomly cut each strip in widths varying from 4" to 7".
2. From multi-color chenille fabric:
   - Cut 2 squares $12^1/4$" x $12^1/4$". Cut each square twice diagonally.
3. From cream cotton fabric:
   - Cut center fabric panel $13^1/2$" x $13^1/2$".
   - Cut 2 backing pieces 25" x 25".
4. From yellow cotton fabric:
   - Cutting on the bias grain of the fabric, cut 4 rectangles 6" x 12".
5. From green cotton fabric:
   - Cutting on the bias grain of the fabric, cut 4 rectangles 6" x 12".

MAKING THE WALL HANGING

Follow Piecing and Pressing, page 85, to make wall hanging.

1. To make chenille flower appliqué, draw lines parallel to the long edges $1/2$" apart on the right side of 1 yellow cotton fabric rectangle. With right sides up, stack all yellow cotton fabric rectangles. Alternating sewing direction, stitch along all drawn lines. Cutting halfway between each stitching line, cut strips apart.
2. Repeat Step 1 for green cotton fabric.
3. With square turned on point, place cream cotton fabric over pattern, page 29. Trace pattern onto panel.

4. To stitch flower appliqué, match stitching line on 1 yellow cotton fabric strip to drawn line on cream cotton fabric panel. Sew strip to fabric panel, backstitching at beginning and end of each strip. To add another strip, stop stitching $1/4$" from end, place new strip under the end; backstitch, and then continue stitching. When stitching a curve, stitch slowly, stopping with needle down; raise presser foot to adjust strip to avoid pleats or puckers.
5. To stitch stem and leaves, repeat Step 4 for green cotton fabric.
6. To fluff chenille, use a spray bottle to wet fabric strips and brush with a stiff-bristle brush.
7. Sew 1 button to center of each flower.
8. Trim center fabric panel to $11^1/2$" x $11^1/2$".
9. Sew multi-color chenille fabric triangles to each side of center fabric panel. Discard remaining triangles.
10. For pieced borders, sew chenille pieces together to form top and bottom borders 5" x $16^1/2$" and 2 side borders 5" x $25^1/2$".
11. Follow **Quilting**, page 88, to mark, layer with batting and backing fabric, and quilt as desired. Our wall hanging was machine quilted in-the-ditch around the cream cotton panel and center square of the wall hanging.
12. Baste pom-pom fringe $1/2$" from edges on right side of wall hanging top.
13. Matching right sides and raw edges, layer wall hanging top on remaining backing fabric. Leaving an opening for turning, sew top to backing through all layers; turn. Slipstitch opening closed.

Wallhanging Diagram

FLOWER-SHAPED PILLOW

SIZE: 12" (30 cm) diameter

FABRIC REQUIREMENTS

Yardage is based on 45"w fabric.

1/2 yd (46 cm) of pink print
1/4 yd (23 cm) of green check
5" x 5" (13 cm x 13 cm) scrap of yellow print

You will also need:

5" x 5" (13 cm x 13 cm) piece of paper-backed fusible web
1 1/4 yds (1.1 m) of pink pom-pom fringe
1 1/4 yds (1.1 m) of purple pom-pom fringe
6" x 9" (15 cm x 23 cm) scrap of cotton batting
12" (30 cm) diameter pillow form
2 assorted yellow buttons

CUTTING OUT THE PIECES

All measurements include a 1/2" seam allowance unless otherwise noted.

1. **From pink print:**
   - For pillow front and back, cut 2 13" diameter circles.
2. **From green print:**
   - Use pattern, page 26, to cut 4 leaves.
3. **From cotton batting:**
   - Use pattern, page 26, to cut 2 leaves.

MAKING THE PILLOW

1. Matching right sides, place 2 leaf pieces together. Layer cotton batting on top. Using a 1/4" seam allowance and leaving straight edge open, sew layers together; turn. Along straight edge, fold a small pleat in leaf; baste. Repeat for remaining leaf pieces.
2. Fuse web to wrong side of yellow print fabric. Cut a 4 1/4" circle from fabric. Fuse circle to center of pillow top front.
3. Staggering pom-poms on fringe so that colors alternate, baste fringe together.
4. Baste fringe to pillow front along 1/2" seam allowance.
5. Baste straight edge of leaves to pillow front over fringe.
6. Matching right sides and leaving an opening for turning, sew pillow front to pillow back; turn. Insert pillow form.
7. With a button on each side of pillow, sew buttons to pillow through center of pillow, pulling tightly to compress center.

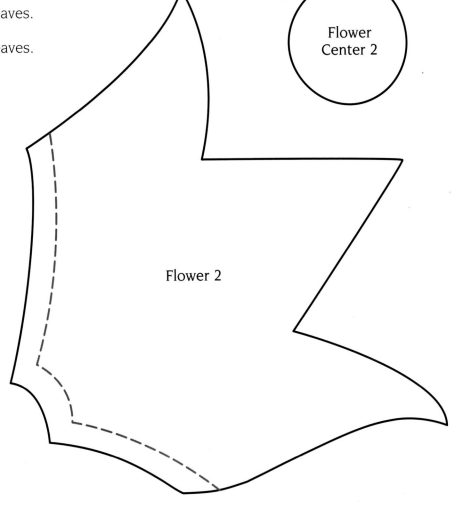

Flower Center 2

Flower 2

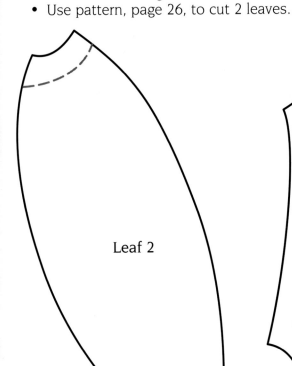

Leaf 2

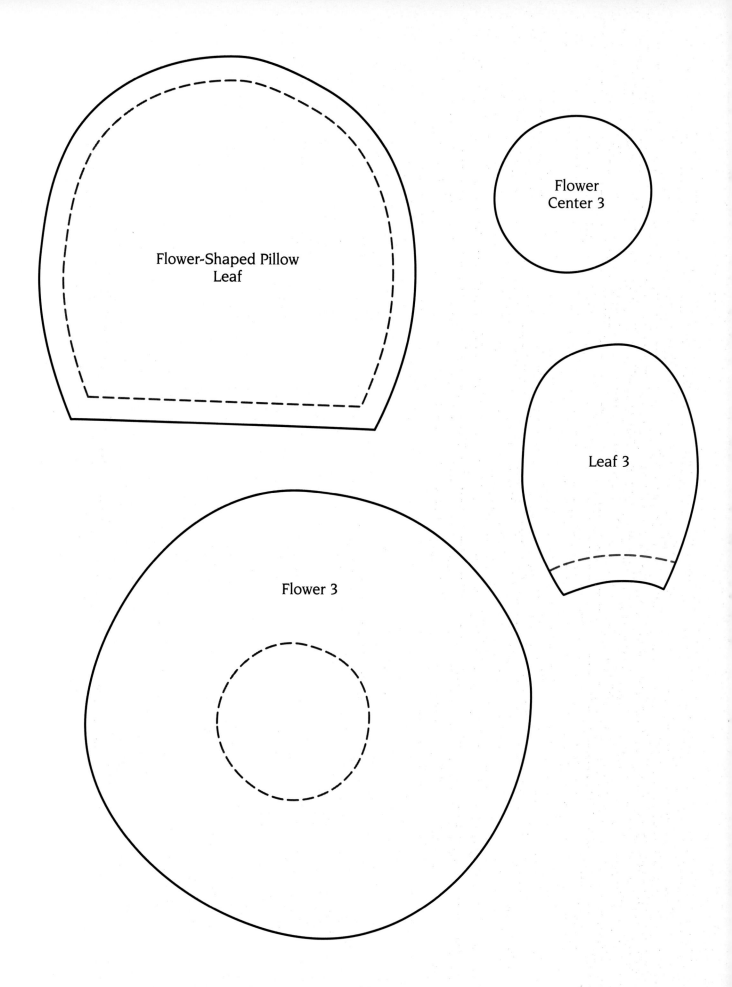

Flower Center 3

Flower-Shaped Pillow
Leaf

Leaf 3

Flower 3

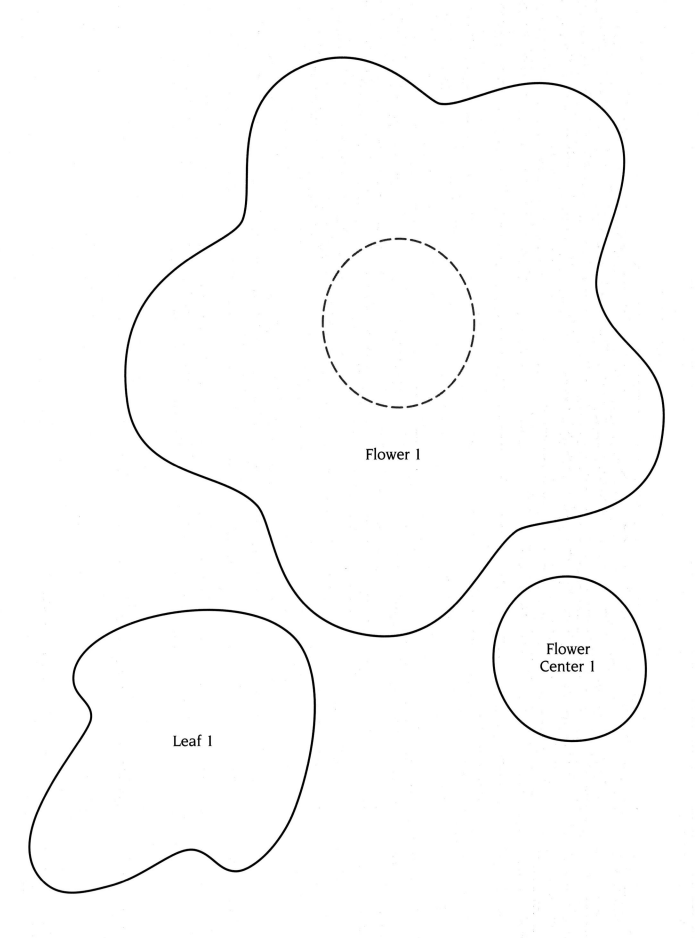

Flower 1

Flower
Center 1

Leaf 1

Flower
Center 4

Flower 4

Leaf 4

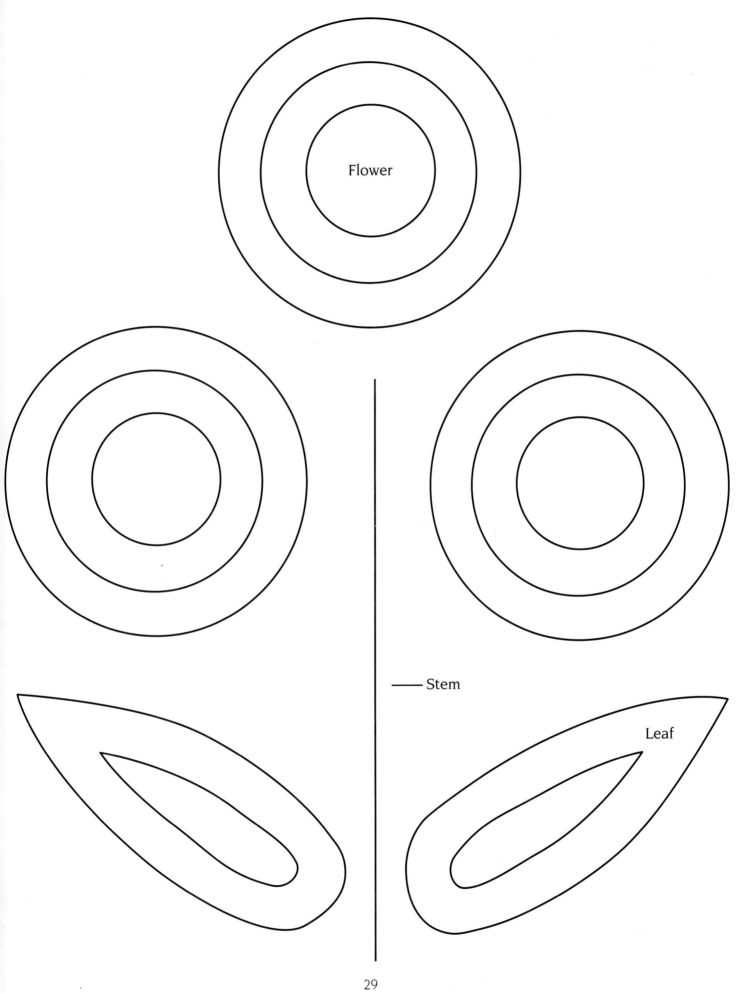

Flower

Stem

Leaf

Grandma's House

Capture forever all the joys of a day spent at Grandma's. An old-fashioned Sawtooth Quilt pattern, cozy appliqués, and easy embroidery are sweet reminders of a home filled with handmade accents. Create a Grandma's House Wall Hanging and a matching pillow. Or use fabric in Grandma's favorite shade of pink to sew the generous bed quilt. Turn the page for more nostalgic accents you'll love.

"What good fortune it is to grow up in a home where there are grandparents." –Suzanne Lafollette

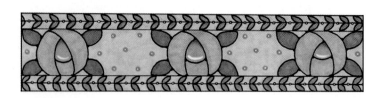

In Grandma's era, combining creativity with frugality was a common practice that yielded wonderful handmade items for home décor. The clean lines of Mary Engelbreit style restate the wise theme of the day in this Stitch in Time Framed Piece, proving that the old adage still holds a lot of truth.

Use traditional embroidery to stitch a garden row of delicate flowers for the center of this Embroidered Pillow (below), then add a button-trimmed border for home-style fashion. Or whip together a batch of gathered circles to create a Petite Yo-yo Pillow (left) that's button-embellished and beautiful to behold.

SAWTOOTH QUILT

QUILT SIZE: 80¹/₂" x 80¹/₂" (204 cm x 204 cm)

Our instructions and diagrams have been adjusted from the antique quilt shown in the photo to ensure accuracy using new techniques, such as rotary cutting and the triangle-square grid method. Our instructions also include traditional double-fold bias binding instead of the facing-style binding used in the original quilt.

FABRIC REQUIREMENTS

Yardage is based on 45"w fabric.

- 4³/₈ yds (4 m) of white solid
- 4 yds (3.7 m) of pink solid
- 8¹/₈ yds (7.4 m) for backing
- 1 yd (91 cm) for binding

You will also need:

- Queen size batting

CUTTING OUT THE PIECES

All measurements include a ¹/₄" seam allowance. Follow **Rotary Cutting**, *page 83.*

1. From white solid:
   - Cut 13 rectangles 16" x 14" for triangle-squares.
   - Cut 1 square 8" x 8".
   - Cut 1 square 19¹/₄" x 19¹/₄". Cut square twice diagonally to make 4 medium triangles.
   - Cut 2 lengthwise top/bottom inner strips 5" x 44".
   - Cut 2 lengthwise side inner strips 5" x 53".
   - Cut 2 lengthwise top/bottom outer strips 5" x 77".
   - Cut 2 lengthwise side inner outer strips 5" x 68".
2. From pink solid:
   - Cut 13 rectangles 16" x 14" for triangle-squares.
   - Cut 2 squares 8³/₈" x 8³/₈". Cut each square once diagonally to make 4 small triangles.
   - Cut 2 squares 21¹/₈" x 21¹/₈". Cut each square once diagonally to make 4 large triangles.
   - Cut 2 lengthwise top/bottom middle strips 5" x 56".
   - Cut 2 side middle strips 5" x 65".

MAKING THE QUILT TOP

Follow **Piecing and Pressing**, *page 85, to make quilt top.*

1. To make triangle-squares, place 1 white and 1 pink rectangle right sides together. Referring to Fig. 1, follow **Making Triangle-Squares**, page 85, to make 60 triangle-squares. Repeat with remaining rectangles to make a total of 780 triangle-squares.

Fig. 1

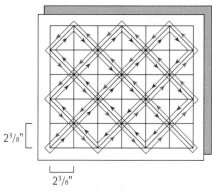

2³/₈"

2³/₈"

Triangle-Square (make 780)

2. Sew 5 triangle-squares together to make Unit 1. Make 2 Unit 1's.

Unit 1 (make 2)

3. Sew 7 triangle-squares together to make Unit 2. Make 2 Unit 2's.

Unit 2 (make 2)

4. Sew 1 Unit 1 to each side of square. Sew 1 Unit 2 to top and bottom of square to make First Square.

First Square

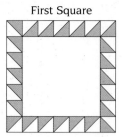

5. Sew 4 small triangles to First Square to make Unit 3.

Unit 3

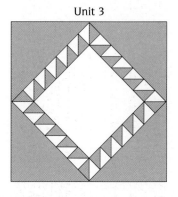

6. Sew 10 triangle-squares together to make Unit 4. Make 2 Unit 4's.

Unit 4 (make 2)

7. Sew 12 triangle-squares together to make Unit 5. Make 2 Unit 5's.

Unit 5 (make 2)

8. Sew 1 Unit 4 to each side of Unit 3. Sew 1 Unit 5 to top and bottom of Unit 3 to make Second Square.

Second Square

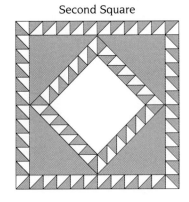

9. Sew 4 medium triangles to Second Square to make Unit 6.

Unit 6

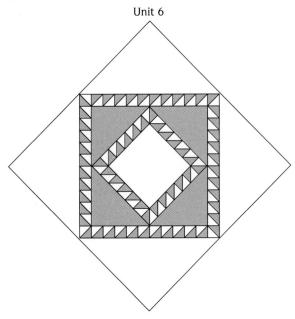

10. Sew 17 triangle-squares together to make Unit 7. Make 2 Unit 7's.

Unit 7 (make 2)

11. Sew 19 triangle-squares together to make Unit 8. Make 2 Unit 8's.

Unit 8 (make 2)

12. Sew 1 Unit 7 to two opposite sides of Unit 6. Sew 1 Unit 8 to remaining sides of Unit 4 to make Third Square.

Third Square

13. Sew 4 large triangles to Third Square to make Unit 9.

Unit 9

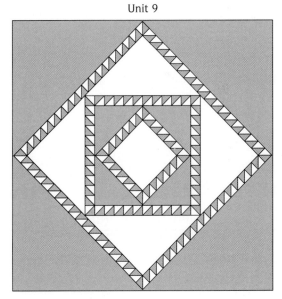

Refer to Quilt Top Diagram page 36, for placement and direction of pieces for Steps 14-24.

14. Sew 27 triangle-squares together to make Unit 10. Make 2 Unit 10's.

15. Sew 29 triangle-squares together to make Unit 11. Make 2 Unit 11's.

16. Sew 1 Unit 10 to top and 1 Unit 10 to bottom of Unit 9. Sew 1 Unit 11 to each side of Unit 9 to make Fourth Square.

17. Sew 1 top inner strip, and 1 bottom inner strip to Fourth Square. Sew 1 side inner strip to each side of Fourth Square to make Unit 12.

18. Sew 35 triangle-squares together to make Unit 13. Make 2 Unit 13's.

19. Sew 37 triangle-squares together to make Unit 14. Make 2 Unit 14's.
20. Sew 1 Unit 13 to top and 1 Unit 13 to bottom of Unit 12. Sew 1 Unit 14 to each side of Unit 12 to make Fifth Square.
21. Sew 1 top middle strip, and 1 bottom middle strip to Fifth Square. Sew 1 side middle strip to each side of Fifth Square to make Unit 15.
22. Sew 43 triangle-squares together to make Unit 16. Make 2 Unit 16's.
23. Sew 45 triangle-squares together to make Unit 17. Make 2 Unit 17's.
24. Sew 1 Unit 16 to top and 1 Unit 16 to bottom of Unit 15. Sew 1 Unit 17 to each side of Unit 15 to make Sixth Square.
25. Sew 1 side outer strip to each side of Sixth Square. Sew 1 top outer strip and 1 bottom outer strip to Sixth Square to make Unit 18.
26. Sew 51 triangle-squares together to make Unit 19. Make 2 Unit 19's.
27. Sew 53 triangle-squares together to make Unit 20. Make 2 Unit 20's.
28. Sew 1 Unit 19 to top and 1 Unit 19 to bottom of Unit 18. Sew 1 Unit 20 to each side of Unit 18 to complete quilt top.

COMPLETING THE QUILT

1. Follow **Quilting**, page 88, to mark layer, and quilt as desired. Our quilt is hand quilted with crosshatching over the entire quilt, except the first (inner) border where a feather pattern was quilted.
2. Cut a 31" square of binding fabric. Follow **Binding**, page 91, to bind quilt using 2¹/₂"w bias binding with mitered corners.

Quilt Top Diagram

GRANDMA'S HOUSE WALL HANGING

SIZE: 29" x 29" (74 cm x 74 cm)

FABRIC REQUIREMENTS

Yardage is based on 45"w fabric.
   1³/₈ yds (1.3 m) of white solid
   ⁵/₈ yd (57 cm) of pink solid
   Assorted print scraps for appliqué
   1 yd (91 cm) for backing
   ¹/₈ yd (11 cm) of black and white stripe
    for binding
You will also need:
   33" x 33" (84 cm x 84 cm) square of batting
   Paper-backed fusible web

CUTTING OUT THE PIECES

Appliqué patterns, pages 40-43, do not include seam allowance and are reversed. Trace appliqué patterns onto fusible web. Follow manufacturer's instructions to fuse web to wrong side of fabric. Trim appliqué pieces along traced lines. All other measurements include a ¹/₄" seam allowance.

1. **From white solid:**
   • Cut 2 rectangles 19" x 14" for triangle-squares.
   • Cut 1 square 8" x 8".
   • Cut 2 squares 13³/₈" x 13³/₈". Cut each square once diagonally to make 4 medium triangles.
2. **From pink solid:**
   • Cut 2 rectangles 19" x 14" for triangle-squares.
   • Cut 1 square 11³/₄" x 11³/₄". Cut square twice diagonally to make 4 small triangles.
3. **From assorted prints for house design appliqués:**
   • Cut pale yellow house.
   • From dark yellow, cut chimney cap, 2 small flower centers, upper windowpane, and lower windowpane.
   • Cut pale blue door.
   • From brown, cut upper window, lower window, and side of door.
   • Cut terra cotta chimney.
   • Cut 2 pink round flowers.
   • Cut 2 green shutters.
   • Cut 4 green check small leaves.
   • Cut dark pink roof.
   • Cut yellow-orange moon.
   • Cut black and white checked ground 7¹/₂" x ⁵/₈".
4. **From assorted prints for heart designs appliqués:**
   • Cut 4 dark pink hearts.
   • Cut 4 dark blue petal flowers.
   • Cut 4 pale yellow large flower centers.
   • Cut 8 green check large leaves.
   • Cut 8 green curlicues.

5. From black and white stripe:
   - Cut 3 strips for single binding 1"w x width of fabric.

MAKING THE WALL HANGING

Follow **Piecing and Pressing***, page 85, to make quilt top. Follow* **Appliqué***, page 87, to add appliqué designs. Refer to photo and* **Wall Hanging Diagram** *for placement of appliqué pieces.*

1. To make triangle-squares, place 1 white and 1 pink rectangle right sides together. Referring to Fig. 1, follow **Making Triangle-Squares**, page 85, to make 70 triangle-squares. Repeat with remaining rectangles to make a total of 140 triangle-squares.

Fig. 1

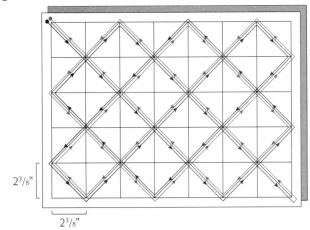

2³/₈"

2³/₈"

Triangle-Square (make 140)

2. Follow Steps 2 – 12 from **Sawtooth Quilt**, pages 34 – 35, to piece wall hanging.

3. Appliqué house design to white center block, and heart designs in each corner white triangle, using Satin Stitch and matching thread. Satin Stitch door hinges and doorknob using brown thread. Add French Knots around appliquéd hearts using 3 strands of black floss.

4. Follow **Quilting**, page 88, to mark layer, and quilt as desired. Our wall hanging is machine quilted in-the-ditch around the triangle-squares, outline quilted around the appliqués with tendrils added to the corner appliqués, and a flower design quilted in the large pink triangles.

5. Sew binding strips together to make continuous straight grain single-fold binding. Follow **Binding**, page 91, to bind quilt with mitered corners.

Wall Hanging Diagram

GRANDMA'S HOUSE PILLOW

SIZE: 11" x 11" (28 cm x 28 cm)

FABRIC REQUIREMENTS

Yardage is based on 45"w fabric.
   ³/₈ yd (34 cm) of white solid
   ³/₈ yd (34 cm) of pink solid
   Assorted print scraps for appliqué
   ¹/₈ yd (11 cm) of black and white stripe for welting
You will also need:
   1¹/₂ yds (1.4 m) ³/₈" (10 mm) cord for welting
   Polyester fiberfill
   Paper-backed fusible web

CUTTING OUT THE PIECES

Appliqué patterns, pages 42-43, do not include seam allowance and are reversed. Trace appliqué patterns onto fusible web. Follow manufacturer's instructions to fuse web to wrong side of fabric. Trim appliqué pieces along traced lines. All other measurements include a ¹/₄" seam allowance.

1. From white solid:
   - Cut 1 rectangle 12" x 10" for triangle-squares.
   - Cut 1 square 8" x 8".
   - Cut 1 square for backing 11" x 11".

2. From pink solid:
   - Cut 1 rectangles 12" x 10" for triangle-squares.

3. From assorted prints for house design appliqué:
   - Cut 1 pale yellow house.
   - From dark yellow, cut chimney cap, 2 small flower centers, upper window pane, and lower window pane.
   - Cut pale blue door.
   - From brown, cut upper window, lower window, and side of door.
   - Cut terra cotta chimney.
   - Cut 2 pink round flowers.
   - Cut 2 green shutters.
   - Cut 4 green check small leaves.
   - Cut dark pink roof.
   - Cut yellow-orange moon.
   - Cut black and white checked ground 7^1/$_2$" x ^{5}/$_8$".
4. From black and white stripe:
   - Cut 2 strips for welting 2"w x width of fabric.

MAKING THE PILLOW

*Follow **Piecing and Pressing**, page 85, to make pillow top. Follow **Appliqué**, page 87, to add appliqué designs. Refer to photo, page 31, for placement of appliqué pieces.*

1. To make triangle-squares, place 1 white and 1 pink rectangle right sides together. Referring to Fig. 1, follow **Making Triangle-Squares**, page 85, to make 24 triangle-squares.

Fig. 1

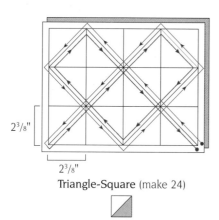

2^3/$_8$"

2^3/$_8$"

Triangle-Square (make 24)

2. Follow Steps 2-4 of Sawtooth Quilt, page 34, to make triangle-squares and sew to 8" x 8" square.
3. Appliqué house design to white center block, using Satin Stitch and matching thread. Satin Stitch door hinges and doorknob using brown thread.
4. Sew welting strips together end-to-end.
5. Follow **Pillow Finishing**, page 95, to complete pillow with welting.

STITCH IN TIME FRAMED PIECE
SIZE: 21" x 20^1/$_4$" (53 cm x 51 cm)

FABRIC REQUIREMENTS
Yardage is based on 45"w fabric.
  ^{1}/$_2$ yd (46 cm) of white solid
  ^{5}/$_8$ yd (57 cm) of pink print
  Assorted pastel print scraps for appliqué
You will also need:
  Embroidery floss: yellow, 2 shades of pink, fuchsia, purple, violet, green, 3 shades of yellow-green, and 2 shades of blue
  1 package of white baby rick rack
  Leaf green acrylic paint
  Paper-backed fusible web

CUTTING OUT THE PIECES
All measurements include a ^{1}/$_4$" seam allowance.
1. **From white solid:**
   - Cut 1 rectangle 15" x 14".
2. **From pink print:**
   - Cut 2 top/bottom borders 5" x 12^5/$_8$".
   - Cut 2 side borders 5" x 20^3/$_4$".

MAKING THE FRAMED PIECE
*Follow **Embroidery Stitches**, page 93 for all embroidery. Follow **Piecing and Pressing**, page 85, to add borders after completing appliqué and embroidery designs.*
1. Use water-soluble pen to trace pattern, pages 44-45, onto white solid rectangle, moving fabric as needed to trace each half.
2. Use a pencil to trace each appliqué pattern onto tracing paper; cut out patterns. Follow manufacturer's instructions to fuse web to wrong side of appliqué fabric. Draw around pattern on right side of appliqué fabrics; cut out appliqués. Fuse appliqués to white rectangle.
3. Using 2 strands of matching floss, add Straight Stitches around each of the letters "NINE" and small appliquéd flowers and leaves. Add Satin Stitch centers with 2 strands of yellow floss to some flowers, and Cross Stitch centers with 3 strands of yellow floss to others. Use 3 strands of dark pink to add petals to the pink flower over "NINE", and 3 strands of dark blue to add petals to the 2 blue flowers with Satin Stitched centers.
4. Use a Running Stitch and 3 strands of dark yellow-green floss to add "STITCH IN TIME SAVES". Add a flower for the dot over the "I" with 6 strands of yellow and a French Knot, and 3 strands of purple and Lazy Daisy Stitches.

5. Stem Stitch stems and leaves of the 3 flowers under the word "NINE" using 3 strands of green floss. Add short Straight Stitches to top of each leaf. Make French Knots with 6 strands of yellow floss for centers of these flowers; add Lazy Daisy Stitches for petals using 3 strands of light pink for first flower, light blue for second, and fuchsia for third.

6. Dye white rick rack using $1/3$ cup water and 1 tablespoon leaf green acrylic paint. Using 3 strands of light yellow-green floss, Couch Stitch baby rick rack for large flower stem and leaves. Make center of large flower with French Knot and 6 strands of yellow floss. Add Stem Stitches in circular pattern around French Knot with 3 strands of yellow floss. Add petals using 6 strands of violet floss and Lazy Daisy Stitches. Add Straight Stitches under flower center using 3 strands of violet floss, 1 French Knot with 6 strands of purple floss, and 1 French Knot with 6 strands of dark yellow green floss.

7. Cross Stitch border square and over appliquéd letter "A" with 4 strands of fuchsia floss. Back Stitch outer edges of border and "A" with 4 strands of purple floss. Add French Knots at corners of each Cross Stitch using 4 strands of yellow floss.

8. Trim appliquéd and embroidered rectangle to $12^5/8$" x $11^3/4$". Add top and bottom borders, then side borders to rectangle.

9. Center design onto cardboard or mounting board. Wrap edges around to back and tape in place, keeping stitched piece straight and taut; insert into frame.

EMBROIDERED PILLOW

SIZE: $15^1/2$" x $12^1/4$" (39 cm x 31 cm)

FABRIC REQUIREMENTS

Yardage is based on 45"w fabric.
   $1/2$ yd (46 cm) of white solid
   $1/8$ yd (11 cm) of green print
   $1/2$ yd (46 cm) of pink print
You will also need:
   Embroidery floss: yellow, fuchsia, purple, violet, and three shades of yellow green
   1 package of white baby rick rack
   Leaf green acrylic paint
   38 assorted white buttons
   Polyester fiberfill

CUTTING OUT THE PIECES

Measurements include a $1/4$" seam allowance, except around outer edge of pillow where a $1/2$" seam allowance is included.

1. **From white solid:**
   • Cut 1 rectangle 14" x 11".
2. **From green print:**
   • Cut 2 top/bottom inner borders $1^1/2$" x 10".
   • Cut 2 side inner borders $1^1/2$" x $8^3/4$".
3. **From pink print:**
   • Cut 2 top/bottom borders $2^3/4$" x 12".
   • Cut 2 side borders $2^3/4$" x $13^1/4$".
   • Cut rectangle $16^1/2$" x $13^1/4$" for pillow back.

MAKING THE PILLOW

Follow Embroidery Stitches, page 93, for all embroidery. Follow Piecing and Pressing, page 85, to add borders after completing appliqué and embroidery designs.

1. Trace pattern, page 41, onto center of white rectangle using water soluble pen.
2. Dye white rick rack using $1/3$ cup water and 1 tablespoon leaf green acrylic paint. Using 3 strands of light yellow-green floss, Couch Stitch baby rick rack for outer flower stems and leaves.
3. Make center of each flower with French Knot and 6 strands of yellow floss. Add Stem Stitches in circular pattern around French Knot with 3 strands of yellow floss. Add petals using 6 strands of violet floss and Lazy Daisy Stitches to outer flowers, and purple floss to center flower. Add Straight Stitches under each outer flower center using 3 strands of violet floss, 1 French Knot with 6 strands of purple floss, and 1 French Knot with 6 strands of dark yellow green floss.
4. Stem Stitch stems and leaves of center flower using 3 strands of medium yellow-green floss. Add short Straight Stitches to top of each leaf.
5. Trim embroidered rectangle to 10" x $6^3/4$". Add top and bottom inner borders, then side inner borders to rectangle. Add top and bottom outer borders, then side outer borders.
6. Sew 11 buttons evenly spaced across each inner top and bottom border and 8 buttons evenly spaced on each side border.
7. With right sides together and using $1/2$" seam allowance, sew pillow top and pillow back together, leaving opening for turning. Clip corners, turn, and stuff with fiberfill; whipstitch opening closed.

PETITE YO-YO PILLOW

SIZE: 10" x 10" (25 cm x 25 cm)

FABRIC REQUIREMENTS

Yardage is based on 45"w fabric.

   ³/₈ yd (34 cm) of white solid
   ¹/₈ yd (23 cm) of green print
   36 different print scraps for yo-yos
   ¹/₈ yd (11 cm) of black and white stripe
    for welting

You will also need:

   1 yd (91 cm) of white medium rick rack
   1¹/₄ yds (1.1 m) of ³/₈" (10 mm) cord for welting
   Polyester fiberfill
   4 novelty buttons

CUTTING OUT THE PIECES

All measurements include a ¹/₄" seam allowance.

1. From white solid:
    *   Cut 1 square 6¹/₄" x 6¹/₄".
    *   Cut 1 square for backing 9³/₄" x 9³/₄".
2. From green print:
    *   Cut 2 side borders 2¹/₄" x 6¹/₄".
    *   Cut 2 top/bottom borders 2¹/₄" x 9³/₄".
3. From each of the different print scraps:
    *   Cut 1 yo-yo from pattern on page 41.
4. From black and white stripe:
    *   Cut 2 strips for welting 2"w x width of fabric.

MAKING THE PILLOW

Follow **P**iecing and **P**ressing, *page 85, to make pillow top.*

1. To make **yo-yo**, turn edge of circle ¹/₄" to wrong side and make a running stitch all around edge using 2 strands of thread (Fig. 1). Pull threads tight from both ends and tie a knot; clip threads (Fig. 2).

Fig. 1

Fig. 2

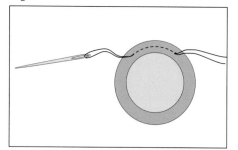
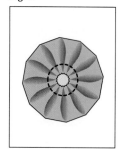

2. Arrange yo-yos so that there is a nice mix of colors throughout. Join yo-yos by placing 2 together front to front. Using thread that blends with fabrics, whipstitch yo-yos together on one side. Join yo-yos into 6 rows of 6; join rows.
3. Sew 1 side border to each side of square. Sew top/bottom borders to pillow top.

4. Sew rick rack to border 1¹/₄" from outer edge, mitering corners. Sew button to each corner.
5. Center yo-yo panel in white center square and whipstitch in place.
6. Sew welting strips together end-to-end.
7. Follow **Pillow Finishing**, page 95, to complete pillow with welting.

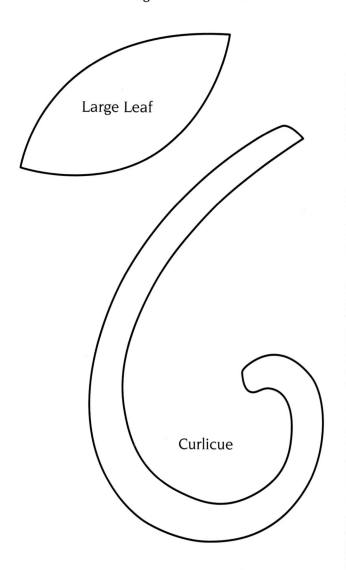

Petal Flower

Large Flower Center

Large Leaf

Curlicue

Heart

Yo-Yo Circle

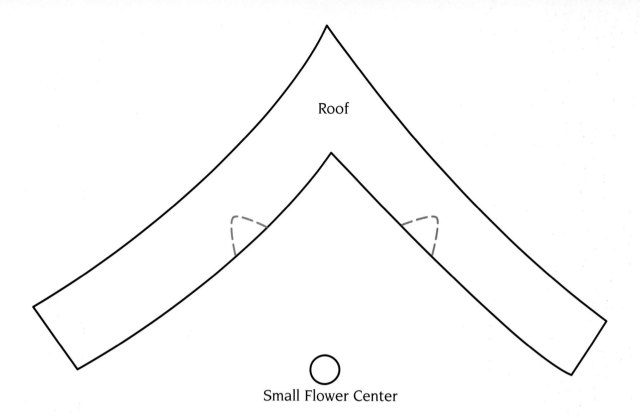

Roof

Small Flower Center

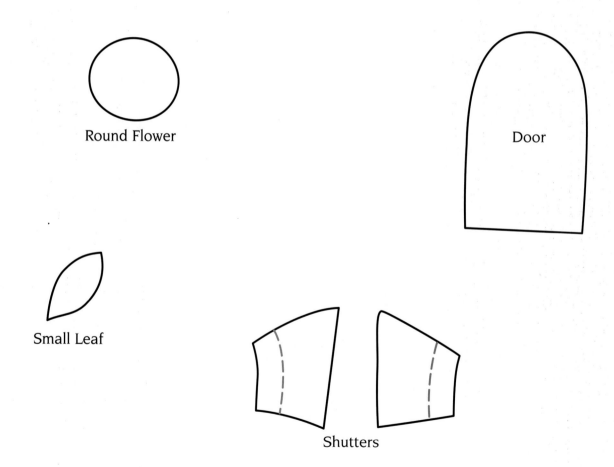

Round Flower

Door

Small Leaf

Shutters

Chimney

Moon

Chimney Cap

Side of Door

Lower Window

House

Lower Windowpane

Upper Windowpane

Upper Window

43

Come Have Tea

ave tea with the Queen of Everything! Mary Engelbreit's fans will recognize her artful style on these terrific kitchen accessories. Quick appliqué and a variety of colorful cloth, including Mary's own cherry fabric, will have your fingers flying through the easy steps to create this playful Tea Time Wall Hanging.

"When we are grown we'll smile and say we had no cares in childhood's day — but we'll be wrong. 'Twill not be true. I've this much care ... I care for you." —Author Unknown

Here's a perky bit of kitchen help for your busy hands. Simple-to-make Nine-Patch and Teacup Potholders and a Teacup Fingertip Towel will remind you that the next comforting cup of tea is just a kettle's whistle away.

47

Everyone should enjoy the luxury of tea time, but these afternoon treats are all yours to savor. Of course a Patchwork Table Runner (below) must have a sprinkling of blossoms to coordinate with the Tea Cozy (opposite). And lest you catch a chill from perching upon a cold chair, pamper yourself with a coordinating Chairback Cover (left).

TEA TIME WALL HANGING

SIZE: 20" x 19" (51 cm x 48 cm)

FABRIC REQUIREMENTS

Yardage is based on 45"w fabric.

$\frac{1}{4}$ yd (23 cm) of cream print

$\frac{1}{4}$ yd (23 cm) of black cherry print

$\frac{1}{4}$ yd (23 cm) each of 4 assorted red prints for border

$\frac{1}{8}$ yd (11 cm) of yellow print for border

Scraps of green, red, yellow, blue, gray, and black prints for appliqués

$\frac{3}{4}$ yd (69 cm) for backing

$\frac{1}{2}$ yd (46 cm) for binding

You will also need:

24" x 23" (61 x 58 cm) square of batting

$\frac{1}{2}$ yd (46 cm) of paper-backed fusible web

CUTTING OUT THE PIECES

Appliqué patterns (pages 55 - 56) do not include seam allowance and are reversed. Trace appliqué patterns onto fusible web. Follow manufacturer's instructions to fuse web to wrong side of fabric. Trim appliqué pieces along traced lines. All other measurements include a $\frac{1}{4}$" seam allowance.

1. From cream print:
   - Cut 1 rectangle 13" x 7$\frac{1}{2}$".
2. From black cherry print:
   - Cut 1 rectangle 13" x 5".
   - Cut 4 border squares 3$\frac{1}{2}$" x 3$\frac{1}{2}$".
3. From yellow print:
   - Cut 2 inner side borders 1" x 12".
   - Cut 2 inner top/bottom borders 1" x 14"
4. From assorted red prints:
   - Cut 2 top/bottom outer borders 3$\frac{1}{2}$" x 14".
   - Cut 2 side outer borders 3$\frac{1}{2}$" x 13".
5. From green, red, yellow, blue, gray, and black prints:
   - Cut 1 each of teapot, teapot spout, spout opening, teapot handle, teapot base, teapot lid, teapot lid rim, teapot lid handle, flower, outer flower center, inner flower center, and spoon.
   - Cut 2 cup handles.
   - Cut 3 each of cups, cup openings, cup bases, saucers, flowers, outer flower centers, and inner flower centers.
   - Cut 6 leaves.

MAKING THE WALL HANGING

*Follow **Piecing and Pressing**, page 85, to make wall hanging. Refer to Wall Hanging Diagram for placement of pieces.*

1. Sew small rectangle and large rectangle together.
2. Arrange, then fuse appliqués to center section of wall hanging. Refer to **Satin Stitch Appliqué**, page 87, to stitch appliqués in place.
3. Sew 1 square to each end of side outer borders.
4. Sew side inner borders, then top and bottom inner borders to center section of wall hanging. Sew outer top and bottom borders, then outer side borders to center section to complete wall hanging top.
5. Follow **Quilting**, page 88, to mark, layer, and quilt as desired. Our wall hanging is machine quilted with stipple quilting in the cream background, in-the-ditch quilting around each of the flowers, and a flower pattern in the outer border.
6. Cut a 15" square of binding fabric. Follow **Binding**, page 91, to bind wall hanging using 2"w double-fold bias binding with mitered corners.

Wall Hanging Diagram

NINE-PATCH POTHOLDER

SIZE: 8" x 8" (20 cm x 20 cm)

FABRIC REQUIREMENTS

Yardage is based on 45"w fabric.

$^3/_8$ yd (34 cm) of black cherry print
4 scraps of assorted yellow prints
4 scraps of assorted red prints

You will also need:

$^3/_8$ yd (34 cm) of fleece for batting

CUTTING OUT THE PIECES

All measurements include a $^1/_4$" seam allowance.

1. From black cherry print:
   • Cut 1 square 8$^1/_2$" x 8$^1/_2$" for backing.
   • Cut 1 small square 2$^1/_2$" x 2$^1/_2$".
   • Cut 2 top/bottom borders 1$^1/_2$" x 8$^1/_2$".
   • Cut 2 side borders 1$^1/_2$" x 6$^1/_2$".
   • Cut 1 strip 2"w for binding and loop.
2. From yellow print scraps:
   • Cut 4 squares 2$^1/_2$" x 2$^1/_2$".
3. From red print scraps:
   • Cut 4 squares 2$^1/_2$" x 2$^1/_2$".
4. From fleece:
   • Cut 3 squares 8$^1/_2$" x 8$^1/_2$".

MAKING THE POTHOLDER

Follow Piecing and Pressing, page 85, to make potholder. Refer to Nine-Patch Potholder Diagram for placement of pieces.

1. Sew 9 squares together to make center section of potholder.
2. Sew side borders to center section of potholder. Sew top/bottom borders to center section to complete potholder top.
3. Layer backing (right side down), 3 batting squares, then potholder top (right side up). Pin or baste all layers together.
4. Press under one long side of binding strip $^1/_4$". Matching raw edges, begin at one corner of top of potholder and attach binding strip, mitering corners. At last corner, leave 5$^1/_2$" of binding strip for loop. Press extended binding strip in half lengthwise with raw edges turned under $^1/_4$"; topstitch through all layers near folded edges.
5. Pin end of extended binding strip to wrong side of potholder forming loop. Blind Stitch binding to back of potholder, catching end of loop in binding.

Nine-Patch Potholder Diagram

TEACUP POTHOLDER

SIZE: 8" x 8" (20 cm x 20 cm)

FABRIC REQUIREMENTS

Yardage is based on 45"w fabric.

Scraps of yellow, green, and blue prints for appliqués
Scrap of black and white check print
Scrap of red polka dot print
$^3/_8$ yd (34 cm) of black cherry print

You will also need:

$^3/_8$ yd (34 cm) of fleece for batting
Paper-backed fusible web

CUTTING OUT THE PIECES

Appliqué patterns, page 55, do not include seam allowance and are reversed. Trace appliqué patterns onto fusible web. Follow manufacturer's instructions to fuse web to wrong side of fabric. Trim appliqué pieces along traced lines. All other measurements include a $^1/_4$" seam allowance.

1. From black cherry print:
   • Cut 1 square 8$^1/_2$" x 8$^1/_2$" for backing.
   • Cut 2 top/bottom outer borders 1$^1/_2$" x 8$^1/_2$".
   • Cut 2 side outer borders 1$^1/_2$" x 6$^1/_2$".
   • Cut 1 strip 2"w for binding and loop.
2. From yellow, green, and blue prints for appliqué:
   • Cut 1 cup, 1 cup handle, 1 cup base, 1 cup opening, and 1 saucer.
3. From red polka dot print:
   • Cut 1 square 5$^1/_2$" x 5$^1/_2$".
4. From black and white check print:
   • Cut 2 side inner borders 1" x 5$^1/_2$".
   • Cut 2 top/bottom inner borders 1$^1/_2$" x 6$^1/_2$".
5. From fleece:
   • Cut 3 squares 8$^1/_2$" x 8$^1/_2$".

MAKING THE POTHOLDER

Follow Piecing and Pressing, page 85, and Appliqué, page 87, to make potholder. Refer to Teacup Potholder Diagram, page 52, for placement of pieces.

1. Appliqué design to center of red polka dot square.
2. Sew side inner borders, then top/bottom inner borders to appliquéd square. Sew side outer borders, then top/bottom outer borders to complete potholder top.
3. Layer backing (right side down), 3 batting squares, then potholder top (right side up). Pin or baste all layers together.

4. Refer to steps 4-5 of Nine-Patch Potholder, page 51, to complete the potholder.

Teacup Potholder Diagram

TEACUP FINGERTIP TOWEL

Size: 16" x 19¹/₂" (41 cm x 50 cm)

FABRIC REQUIREMENTS

Yardage is based on 45"w fabric.
- ¹/₂ yd (48 cm) of red print
- ¹/₄ yd (23 cm) of gold print
- ¹/₈ yd (11 cm) of green print
- Scraps of green, red, yellow, blue, and black prints for appliqués
- Paper-backed fusible web

CUTTING OUT THE PIECES

Appliqué patterns, page 57, do not include seam allowance and are reversed. Trace appliqué patterns onto fusible web. Follow manufacturer's instructions to fuse web to wrong side of fabric. Trim appliqué pieces along traced lines. All other measurements include a ¹/₄" seam allowance.

1. **From red print:**
   - Cut 1 large rectangle 16¹/₂" x 39¹/₂".
2. **From gold print:**
   - Cut 1 small rectangle 16¹/₂" x 7".
3. **From green print:**
   - Cut 1 strip 16¹/₂" x 1¹/₂".
4. **From green, red, yellow, blue, and black prints:**
   - Cut 1 each of cup, cup opening, cup base, cup handle, saucer, and napkin.

MAKING THE TOWEL

*Follow **Piecing and Pressing**, page 85, to make towel. Refer to Towel Diagram for placement of pieces.*

1. Sew large rectangle, strip, and small rectangle together along 16¹/₂" edges to make loop.
2. With right sides together, fold towel so gold/red seam falls to the back and lines up with gold/green seam on front. Stitch sides of loop, leaving opening for turning. Turn right side out; whipstitch opening closed.

3. Arrange, then fuse appliqués to towel. Refer to **Satin Stitch Appliqué**, page 87, to stitch appliqués in place.

Towel Diagram

TEA COZY

FABRIC REQUIREMENTS

Yardage is based on 45"w fabric.
- ¹/₂ yd (46 cm) of blue print
- ⁵/₈ yd (57 cm) of black check print
- Scraps of green, red, yellow, blue, and black prints for appliqués

You will also need:
- ¹/₂ yd (46 cm) of fusible fleece
- Paper-backed fusible web

CUTTING OUT THE PIECES

Appliqué patterns, pages 55 and 56, do not include seam allowance and are reversed. Trace appliqué patterns onto fusible web. Follow manufacturer's instructions to fuse web to wrong side of fabric. Trim appliqué pieces along traced lines. All other measurements include a ¹/₄" seam allowance.

1. **From blue print:**
   - Cut 4 **rectangles** 16" x 11".
2. **From black check print:**
   - Cut 2 short binding strips 2¹/₂" x 16".
   - Cut 1 long binding strip 2¹/₂" x 26".
3. **From green, red, yellow, blue, and black prints:**
   - Cut 1 each of teapot, teapot spout, spout opening, teapot handle, teapot base, teapot lid, teapot lid rim, teapot lid handle, flower, outer flower center, and inner flower center.
   - Cut 2 leaves.
4. **From fusible fleece:**
   - Cut 2 **rectangles** 16" x 11".

MAKING THE TEA COZY

Refer to Tea Cozy Diagram for placement of appliqué pieces.

1. Fuse 1 fleece rectangle to wrong side of 1 blue rectangle (front lining). Fuse web to wrong side of 1 blue rectangle (front); remove paper backing. With wrong sides together, fuse lining and front together. Repeat with remaining rectangles to make cozy back.
2. Using cozy pattern, page 59, cut cozy front and cozy back from fused rectangles.
3. Arrange, then fuse appliqué pieces to cozy front and follow **Satin Stitch Appliqué**, page 87, to stitch appliqués in place.
4. Press binding strips in half lengthwise. Follow **Binding**, page 91, to add straight grain binding (short binding strip) to bottom of each cozy piece; trim ends even with cozy. Pin front and back of cozy together (right sides out), and bind around remaining raw edge (long binding strip).

Tea Cozy Diagram

PATCHWORK TABLE RUNNER

SIZE: 16" x 52" (41 cm x 132 cm)

FABRIC REQUIREMENTS

Yardage is based on 45"w fabric.

$5/8$ yd (57 cm) of black check print
$3/8$ yd (34 cm) of red polka dot print
$1/2$ yd (46 cm) total of assorted green, yellow, black, and red prints
Scraps of green, red, yellow, and blue prints for appliqués
$1 5/8$ yds (1.5 m) for backing

You will also need:

$1 5/8$ yds (1.5 m) of batting
Paper-backed fusible web

CUTTING OUT THE PIECES

Appliqué patterns, page 58, do not include seam allowance and are reversed. Trace appliqué patterns onto fusible web. Follow manufacturer's instructions to fuse web to wrong side of fabric. Trim appliqué pieces along traced lines. All other measurements include a $1/4$" seam allowance.

1. From black check print:
   - Cut 2 side borders $2^1/2$" x $36^1/2$".
   - Cut 1 square $12^1/4$" x $12^1/4$". Cut square once diagonally to make 2 large triangles.
2. From red polka dot print:
   - Cut 1 square $10^1/2$" x $10^1/2$". Cut square once diagonally to make 2 small triangles.
3. From assorted green, yellow, black, and red prints:
   - Cut 27 squares $4^1/2$" x $4^1/2$".
4. From green, red, yellow, and blue prints:
   - Cut 18 leaves.
   - Cut 9 petal rings.
   - Cut 9 inner flower centers.
   - Cut 9 outer flower centers.

MAKING THE TABLE RUNNER

*Follow **Piecing and Pressing**, page 85, to make table runner. Refer to Table Runner Diagram for placement of pieces.*

1. Sew 3 squares together to make Row. Make 9 Rows.
2. Sew Rows together to make center section of table runner.
3. Arrange, then fuse appliqué pieces in place, but **do not** stitch.
4. Add side borders to center section.
5. Hem short sides of small triangles, turning under $1/4$" twice.
6. Matching raw edges of long sides and with right sides up, layer 1 large triangle and 1 small triangle. Sew triangles to one end of table runner. Repeat to add 1 large triangle and 1 small triangle to remaining end of table runner.
7. Using pieced table runner top for pattern, cut batting and backing same size.
8. Layer table runner top (right side up), batting, and backing (right side down). Sew around edge, leaving opening for turning.
9. Turn table runner right side out, and press; whipstitch opening closed.
10. Refer to **Satin Stitch Appliqué**, page 87, to stitch appliqués in place sewing through all layers of table runner.

Patchwork Table Runner Diagram

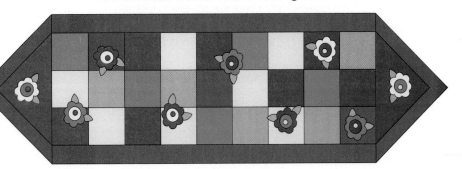

CHAIRBACK COVER

FABRIC REQUIREMENTS

Yardage is based on 45"w fabric.

$1/2$ yd (46 cm) of black check print
$3/8$ yd (34 cm) of red polka dot print
$1/4$ yd (23 cm) of black stripe print
$3/8$" yd (34 cm) total of assorted green, yellow, black, and red prints
Scraps of green, red, yellow, and blue prints for appliqués
1 yd (91 cm) for backing

You will also need:

1 yd (91 m) of batting
Paper-backed fusible web

CUTTING OUT THE PIECES

Appliqué patterns, page 58, do not include seam allowance and are reversed. Trace appliqué patterns onto fusible web. Follow manufacturer's instructions to fuse web to wrong side of fabric. Trim appliqué pieces along traced lines. All other measurements include a $1/4$" seam allowance.

1. **From black check print:**
   - Cut 2 side borders $2^1/2$" x $16^1/2$".
   - Cut 1 square $12^1/4$" x $12^1/4$". Cut square once diagonally to make 2 large triangles.
2. **From red polka dot print:**
   - Cut 1 square $10^1/2$" x $10^1/2$". Cut square once diagonally to make 2 small triangles.
3. **From black stripe print:**
   - Cut 2 strips $2^1/2$"w by width of fabric. Cut strips in half to make 4 (21" long) strips for ties.
4. **From assorted green, yellow, black, and red prints:**
   - Cut 12 squares $4^1/2$" x $4^1/2$".
5. **From green, red, yellow, and blue prints:**
   - Cut 6 leaves.
   - Cut 3 flowers.
   - Cut 3 inner flower centers.
   - Cut 3 outer flower centers.

MAKING THE CHAIRBACK COVER

*Follow **Piecing and Pressing**, page 85, to make chairback cover. Refer to Chairback Cover Diagram for placement of pieces.*

1. Sew 3 squares together to make Row. Make 4 Rows.
2. Sew Rows together to make center section of chairback cover.
3. Arrange, then fuse appliqué pieces in place, but **do not** stitch.
4. Sew side borders to center section.

5. Hem short sides of small triangles, turning under twice $1/4$".
6. Matching raw edges of long sides and with right sides up, layer 1 small triangle and 1 large triangle. Sew to top of chairback cover. Repeat to add 1 small triangle and 1 large triangle to bottom of chairback cover.
7. Using pieced chairback cover top for pattern, cut batting and backing same size.
8. With right sides together, fold 1 strip for tie in half lengthwise. Sew long side with raw edges and 1 short side together. Turn and press to make tie. Repeat to make 4 ties. Pin or tack ties at side corners of chairback cover top.
9. Layer chairback cover (right side up), batting, and backing (right side down). Sew around edge, leaving opening for turning.
10. Turn chairback cover right side out, and press; whipstitch opening closed.
11. Refer to **Satin Stitch Appliqué**, page 87, to stitch appliqués in place sewing through all layers of chairback cover.

Chairback Cover Diagram

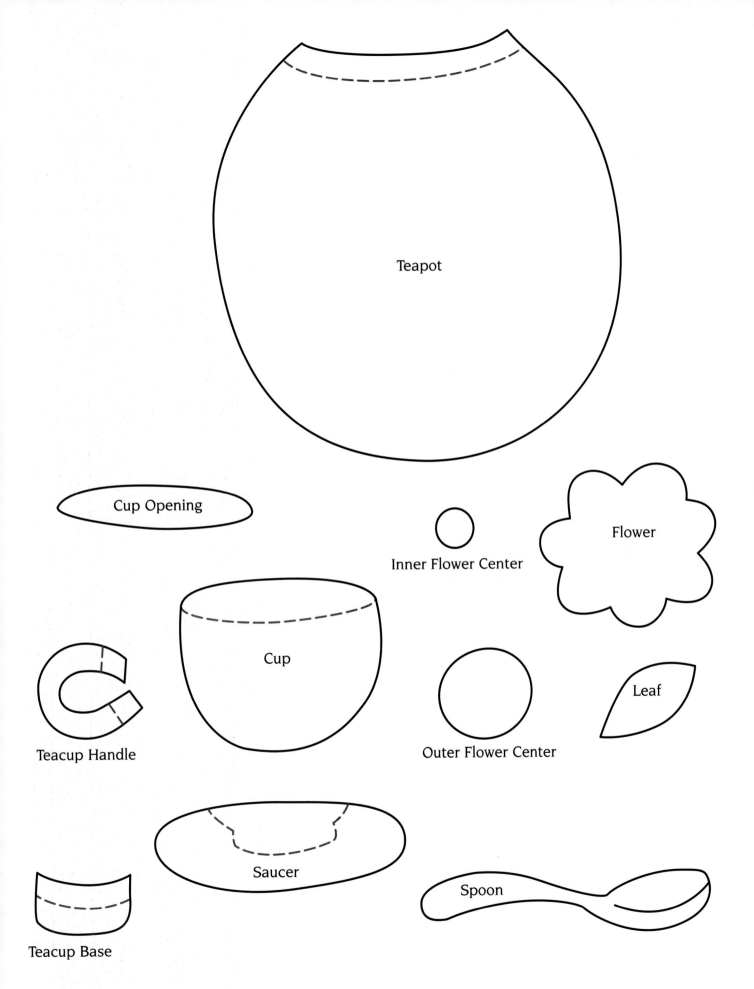

Teapot

Cup Opening

Inner Flower Center

Flower

Cup

Teacup Handle

Outer Flower Center

Leaf

Saucer

Spoon

Teacup Base

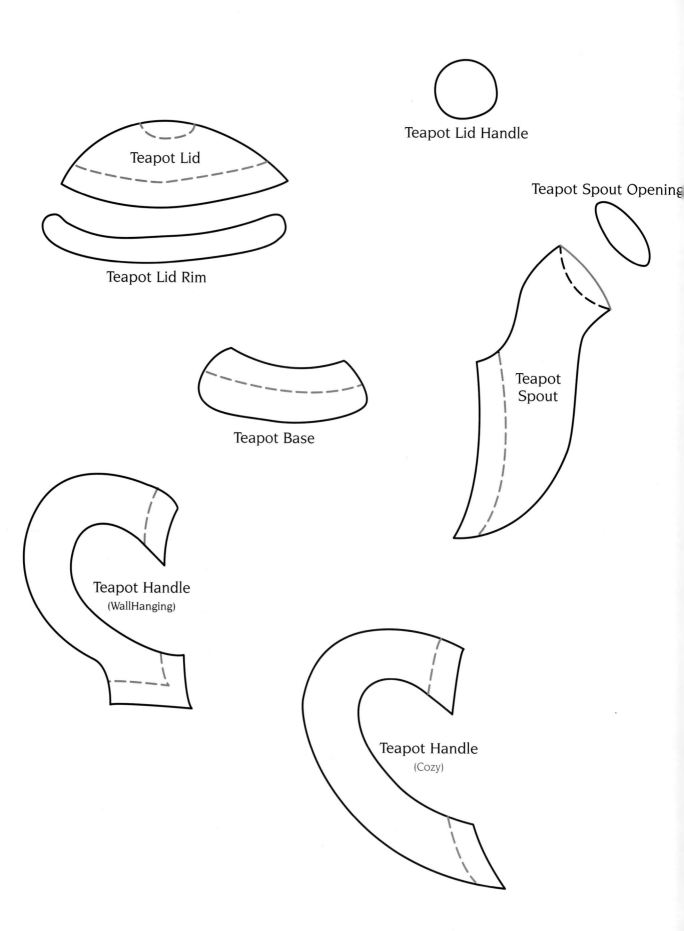

Teapot Lid Handle

Teapot Lid

Teapot Spout Opening

Teapot Lid Rim

Teapot Base

Teapot Spout

Teapot Handle
(WallHanging)

Teapot Handle
(Cozy)

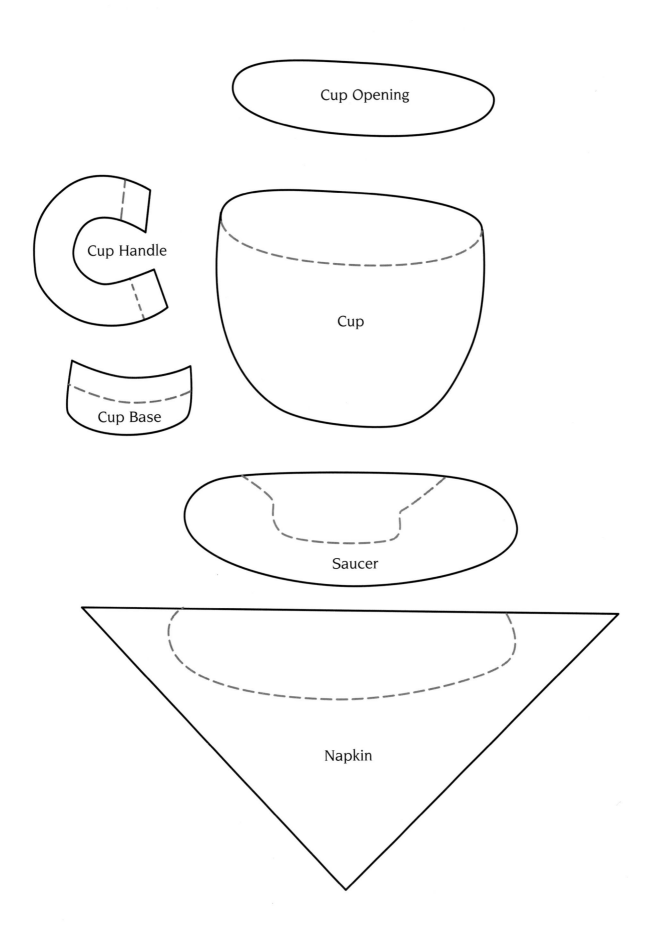

Cup Opening

Cup Handle

Cup

Cup Base

Saucer

Napkin

Inner Flower Center

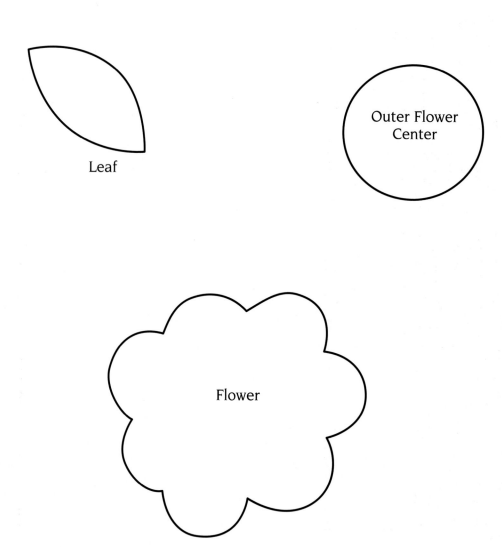

Leaf

Outer Flower
Center

Flower

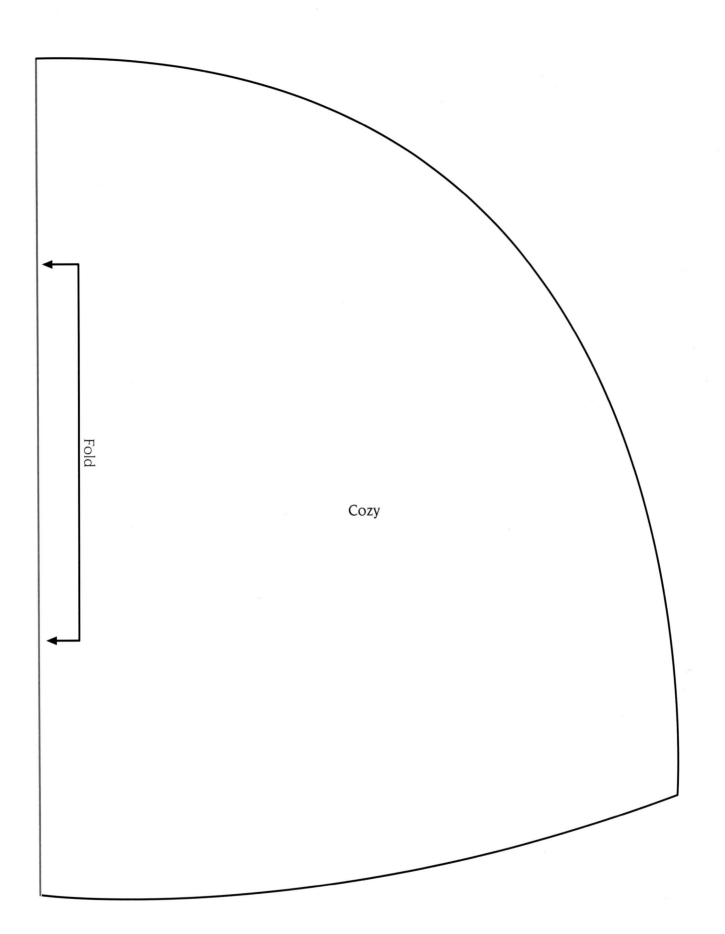

Fold

Cozy

Paper Dolls

Oh, the thrill of your first paper dolls! Remember that tingle of excitement as you put scissors to paper and dreamed of all the fashions your little fingers would create? Mary's own Ann Estelle brings back the joy of childhood on a Paper Doll Wall Hanging that you can make in a jiffy with your grown-up hands.

Make a stuffed figure of Ann Estelle and keep her cozy in the pocket of this ruffled Paper Doll Pillow (above). Ann Estelle also gives a shy smile from this handy Paper Doll Tote Bag (right). Rickrack borders the printed fabric panel and Mary Engelbreit flower buttons add dimension to the bag.

PAPER DOLL WALL HANGING

SIZE: 22" x 13½" (56 cm x 34 cm)

FABRIC REQUIREMENTS

Yardage is based on 45"w fabric.
⅛ yd (11 cm) of green print
⅛ yd (11 cm) of pink check
⅝ yd (57 cm) of white solid
You will also need:
2 yds (1.8 m) green jumbo rickrack
1⅜ yds (1.3 m) green baby rickrack
18" x 26½" (46 cm x 67 cm) cotton batting
Photo transfer paper for color copiers **or** for inkjet printers
14 assorted white buttons
Embroidery floss: green and pink

CUTTING OUT THE PIECES

All measurements include a ¼" seam allowance unless otherwise noted.
1. From green print:
   • Cut 2 side borders 2½" x 10".
   • Cut 2 top/bottom borders 2½" x 22½".
2. From pink check:
   • Cut 4 sashing/borders 1½" x 8".
   • Cut 2 top/bottom borders 1½" x 18½".
3. From white solid:
   • Cut 1 fabric panel 7½" x 10".
   • Cut 2 fabric panels 7" x 10".
   • Cut backing 14" x 22½".

MAKING THE WALL HANGING

*Follow **Piecing** and **Pressing**, page 85, to make wall hanging.*
1. Follow manufacturer's instructions to transfer paper doll art, pages 64-65, to larger white fabric panel. Centering paper doll, trim panel to 5½" x 8". Transfer clothing art to remaining white fabric panels. Centering clothing, trim panels to 5" x 8".
2. Sew transferred panels and 2 sashing strips together to make wall hanging top.
3. Sew short pink checked borders to each side of wall hanging top.
4. Sew remaining pink checked borders to top and bottom of wall hanging top.
5. Repeat Steps 3-4 with green print borders.
6. Baste center of jumbo rickrack ¼" from edges of wall hanging top.
7. Place backing, right side up, on flat surface. Place wall hanging top, right side down, on backing. Layer batting on top. Leaving an opening for turning, sew layers together; turn. Slipstitch opening closed.

8. Using pink floss, sew 5 white buttons to each pink check sashing and sew 1 white button to each corner of pink check border.
9. Using 4 strands of green floss, Backstitch stems on flowers and add Lazy Daisy Stitches for leaves.
10. Sew baby rickrack along inside edge of pink check border approximately ⅛" from inside edge.

PAPER DOLL TOTE BAG

FABRIC REQUIREMENTS

Yardage is based on 45"w fabric.
½ yd (45.7 cm) of green check
⅜ yd (34.3 cm) of white solid
You will also need:
⅞ yd (80 cm) green jumbo rickrack
Photo transfer paper for color copiers or for inkjet printers
5 assorted novelty buttons

CUTTING OUT THE PIECES

All measurements include a ¼" seam allowance unless otherwise noted.
1. From green check:
   • Cut 1 rectangle 11½" x 28½".
   • For handles, cut 2 strips 2½" x 16".
2. From white solid:
   • Cut 1 rectangle 11½" x 28½" for lining.
   • Cut 1 rectangle 7½" x 10" for fabric panel.

MAKING THE TOTE BAG

1. Make a color copy of paper doll and clothing art, pages 64-65. Cut out clothing, removing tabs, then adhere clothing to doll copy. Make a copy of the dressed doll. Follow manufacturer's instructions to transfer paper doll to white fabric panel. Centering paper doll, trim panel to 5½" x 8". Press each side of fabric panel ¼" to wrong side.
2. With top edge 2¾" from one short edge, center fabric panel on green check rectangle; pin in place. Position rickrack under edges of fabric panel, mitering corners and folding raw end to wrong side. Topstitch rectangle and rickrack in place.
3. Matching right sides, sew tote bag front and back together along side edges. Trim bottom corner seam allowances diagonally; press seam allowances open. Do not turn right side out.

4. To form bottom corners of tote bag, match side seams to center bottom; sew across each corner 1¹/₂" from end (Fig. 1). Turn tote bag right side out.

Fig. 1

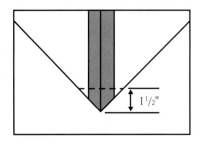

5. Matching right side, fold handle in half lengthwise; sew. Turn right side out.
6. Matching raw edges, pin each end of one handle to right side of tote bag front 2¹/₄" from each side seam, making sure handle is not twisted. Repeat to pin second handle to tote bag back. Sew handles to tote bag.
7. Press top edge of tote bag ¹/₂" to wrong side.
8. Repeat Steps 3-4 to sew lining pieces together and form bottom corners. Press top edge of lining ³/₄" to wrong side. Do not turn lining right side out.
9. Matching wrong sides and side seams, place lining inside tote bag. With handles extended above top of tote bag, slipstitch lining to tote bag ¹/₄" below top edge.
10. Sew buttons to front of tote bag.

PAPER DOLL PILLOW

SIZE: 10" x 10" (25 cm x 25 cm)

FABRIC REQUIREMENTS
Yardage is based on 45"w fabric.
⅝ yd (57 cm) of green floral print
⅜ yd (34 cm) of green check
¹/₂ yd (46 cm) of pink check
Two 3¹/₂" x 7" (9 cm x 18 cm) scraps of white solid
You will also need:
Photo transfer paper for color copiers **or** for inkjet printers
Polyester fiberfill
1¹/₄ yds (1.1 m) of ¹/₄" (7 mm) diameter cord
Three ⁷/₁₆" (11 mm) diameter white buttons
3 assorted novelty buttons

CUTTING OUT THE PIECES
All measurements include a ¹/₄" seam allowance unless otherwise noted.
1. From green floral print:
   • For pillow back, cut 1 square 10¹/₂" x 10¹/₂".
   • Using pattern, page 64, cut pocket.
   • For ruffle, cut a strip 5¹/₂" x 80" (pieced as necessary).
2. From green check:
   • For pillow front, cut 1 square 10¹/₂" x 10¹/₂".
3. From pink check:
   • For cording, cut 1 bias strip 2" x 45" (pieced as necessary).
   • For pocket trim, cut 1 rectangle 1¹/₄" x 4⁷/₈".

MAKING THE PILLOW
1. For doll, follow manufacturer's instructions to transfer paper doll art, page 65, to 1 white fabric scrap. Matching right sides and leaving bottom edge open for turning, sew paper doll transfer to remaining white scrap, approximately ¹/₄" from design. Trim and clip seam allowances; turn.
2. Stuff paper doll shape with fiberfill; slipstitch opening closed.
3. Matching right sides, place 1 long edge of pocket trim ¹/₂" below top edge of pocket. Stitch ¹/₄" from long edge of pocket trim. Fold pocket trim to right side and press. Fold upper edge of pocket trim to wrong side of pocket; topstitch in place. Press side and bottom edges of pocket ¹/₄" to wrong side.
4. Centering pocket and placing top edge 5¹/₄" from one edge of pillow top, topstitch pocket in place.
5. Refer to **Pillow Finishing**, page 95, to add welting and ruffle to pillow top and to finish pillow.
6. Sew white buttons to pocket trim. Sew novelty buttons to pillow top.

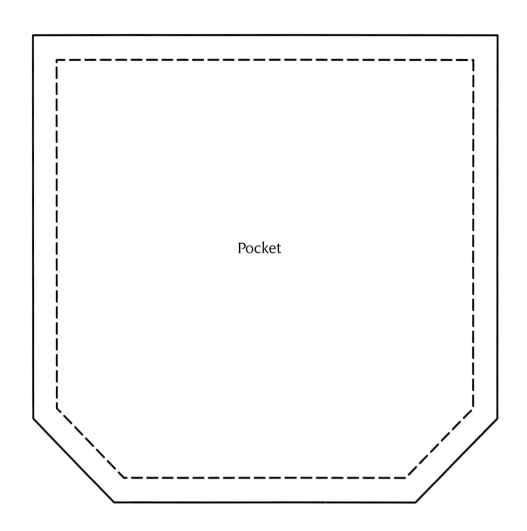

Pocket

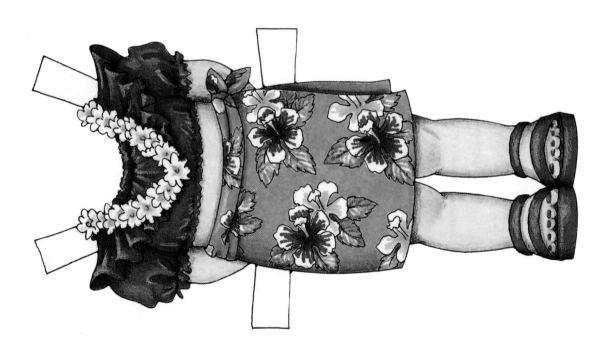

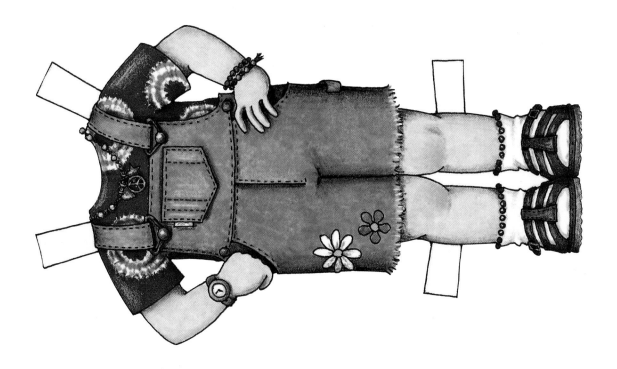

A Very "Mary" Christmas

Get ready for a heartfelt holiday! These "Mary" Christmas Felt Stockings will have little folks standing on their toes to see the goodies hidden inside. Grown-ups will love the fun shapes, too. After all, what could be more jolly than Christmas with Mary Engelbreit?

Looking out from this Kris Kringle Wall Hanging (opposite) and dressed in his best felt finery, Santa wishes you the happiest of Yuletides. And you can create ornaments like these classic Mary Engelbreit shapes (left and below) in a twinkling. Make Candy Cane, Star, Peppermint, and Flower Ornaments to brighten the holidays of all your loved ones!

"Do all the good you can. By all the means you can. In all the ways you can. At all the times you can. To all the people you can. As long as ever you can." —John Wesley

KRIS KRINGLE WALL HANGING

SIZE: 17" x 23³/₈" (43 cm x 59 cm)

FABRIC REQUIREMENTS

Yardage is based on 60"w felt. Felt is also available in 9" x 12" precut pieces.

⁵/₈ yd (57 cm) of black felt
¹/₂ yd (46 cm) of red felt
¹/₂ yd (46 cm) of white felt
9" x 12" piece of lime green felt
9" x 12" piece of light red felt
9" x 12" piece of dark red felt
9" x 12" piece of brown felt
9" x 12" piece of flesh felt
Scrap of gold felt

You will also need:

58 red ³/₈" (10 mm) buttons
Fabric glue
Embroidery floss: green, black, salmon,
  red, brown, and white
1 yd of 1"w red polka dot ribbon
Decorative candy cane or 21" length
  of 1" diameter dowel rod

CUTTING OUT THE PIECES

Patterns are on pages 74 -77.

1. **From black felt:**
   - Cut 1 rectangle 17" x 23³/₈".
2. **From red felt:**
   - Cut 2 side borders 2¹/₂" x 23³/₈".
   - Cut 2 top/bottom borders 2¹/₂" x 17".
   - Cut 1 headband.
   - Cut 1 mouth.
   - Cut 1 left sleeve and 1 right sleeve.
   - Cut 2 flower outer centers.
   - Cut 1 left glove and 1 right glove.
   - Cut 1 coat bottom on fold.
   - Cut 2 legs.
3. **From white felt:**
   - Cut 1 left sleeve trim and 1 right sleeve trim.
   - Cut 1 coat bottom trim.
   - Cut 1 beard.
   - Cut 1 leg trim.
   - Cut 1 mustache.
   - Cut 1 left side hair and 1 right side hair.
   - Cut 2 side border trims.
   - Cut 2 top/bottom border trims.
4. **From lime green felt:**
   - Cut 3 each of holly leaf A and holly leaf B.
   - Cut 2 flower leaves A.
   - Cut 2 flower leaves B.
   - Cut 6 cherry leaves.
5. **From light red felt:**
   - Cut 1 left flower and 1 right flower.
   - Cut 11 cherries.
6. **From dark red felt:**
   - Cut 1 body on fold.
7. **From brown felt:**
   - Cut 1 left shoe and 1 right shoe.
8. **From flesh felt:**
   - Cut 1 face.
9. **From gold felt:**
   - Cut 2 flower inner centers.

MAKING THE WALL HANGING

*Refer to photo, page 68, for placement of pieces. Follow **Embroidery Stitches**, page 93, for all embroidery. Because some of the embroidery will be added after pieces are glued together, use glue sparingly and allow to dry.*

1. Glue top/bottom borders to edges of black rectangle. Glue side borders to rectangle, overlapping ends of top/bottom borders.
2. To add flowers to border trims, attach buttons using black thread and add Lazy Daisy Stitches using 2 strands of green floss for leaves. Glue top/bottom border trims, then side border trims to border.
3. Stem Stitch nose, eyebrows and ear details to face using 3 strands of black floss. Satin Stitch eyes using 3 strands of black floss; add highlight to each eye with French Knot and 6 strands of white floss. If desired, brush a small amount of powdered blush to cheeks and nose.
4. Glue left inner flower center to outer flower center. Make grid pattern in inner flower center with Straight Stitches and Couching at intersections of Straight Stitches, using 2 strands of red floss. Blanket Stitch around inner flower center using 2 strands of black floss. Straight Stitch stripes in outer flower center using 3 strands of white floss. Glue outer flower center to left flower. Blanket Stitch around flower using 2 strands of black floss. Add French Knots to leaf A. Add "plaid" pattern to 1 leaf B with Straight Stitches and Couching at intersections of Straight Stitches, using 2 strands of green floss. Add Couched circles, with a French Knot in each circle, using 2 strands of green floss, to another leaf B. Blanket Stitch around leaves using 2 strands of green floss. Glue leaves and flower to left sleeve.
5. Complete right sleeve in the same manner as left sleeve.

6. Using Straight Stitches, add grid pattern to cherries using 2 strands of salmon floss. Using 2 strands of green floss, add French Knots to half of cherry leaves, and Straight Stitches to remainder of cherry leaves. Glue cherry leaves and cherries to coat bottom. Add cherry stems and veins to leaves using Stem Stitch and 3 strands of black floss.

7. Add details to shoes with Stem Stitch and 4 strands of brown floss.

8. Add stripes to legs with Stem Stitch and French Knots, using 3 strands of black floss.

9. Arrange shoes, legs, body, bottom of coat, sleeves, hair, and face onto black background; glue into place. Glue beard, mouth, then mustache into place. Glue headband and 6 holly leaves to top of head. Glue gloves and trim into place.

10. For ties, cut ribbon into 4 equal lengths. Glue ribbon ties to top of wall hanging, and tie to dowel rod or decorative candy cane (**Note**: We removed the hook from our candy cane).

STOCKING WITH HANGING ORNAMENTS

FABRIC REQUIREMENTS
Yardage is based on 60"w felt. Felt is also available in 9" x 12" precut pieces.

$3/8$ yd (34 cm) of white felt
$3/8$ yd (34 cm) of red felt
Scraps of green, gold, and pink felt

You will also need:

9 red $3/8$" (10 mm) buttons
10 white $3/8$" (10 mm) buttons
White $5/8$" (16 mm) button
Green embroidery floss
Small piece of paper-backed fusible web
4 small red wooden beads
8 white and 8 gold small flat wooden beads
Clear monofilament thread

CUTTING OUT THE PIECES
Patterns are on pages 78-80.

1. From white felt:
   • Cut 1 stocking using outer line.
   • Cut 2 small candy canes.
   • Cut 2 small peppermint flowers.
   • Cut 2 large peppermint flowers.
   • Cut 2 stocking cuffs.
   • Cut 2 strips $1/2$" x 6" using pinking shears.

2. From red felt:
   • Cut 1 stocking using inner line.
   • Cut 1 strip $5/8$" x 9" for hanger.
   • Cut 7 small candy cane stripes.
   • Cut 4 large peppermint stripes.
   • Cut 4 small peppermint stripes.

3. From green felt:
   • Cut 1 toe.
   • Cut 1 heel.
   • Cut 2 large rounded leaves.
   • Cut 2 small rounded leaves.
   • Cut 3 small pointed leaves.

4. From gold felt:
   • Cut 2 small stars.
   • Cut 1 large peppermint center.
   • Cut 1 small peppermint center.
   • Cut 1 pink flower center.

5. From pink felt:
   • Cut 2 pink flowers.

MAKING THE STOCKING
Refer to photo, page 67, for placement of pieces.

1. Follow instructions on page 73 to make 1 **Peppermint Ornament**.

2. To make stocking, refer to steps 2-6 of **Stocking with Attached Ornaments**, page 72.

3. Glue **Peppermint Ornament** to cuff using fabric glue.

4. Arrange 3 small pointed leaves on 1 pink flower. Glue second pink flower to top, securing leaves in place. Glue center to flower. Add veins to leaves and petals to flower using black permanent marker.

5. Glue 2 small candy canes together. Glue red stripes in place, and add small stripes between felt stripes using red permanent marker.

6. Glue 2 small stars together. Sew a large white button and a small red button, stacked, to center of star. Follow **Making a Tassel**, page 96, to make tassel with green embroidery floss, running tassel ties through gold bead with embroidery needle. Run tassel ties between layers of star and out back at center of star; tie off.

7. Arrange 2 small rounded leaves to 1 small peppermint. Glue second small peppermint to top, securing leaves in place. Glue stripes to flower, then flower center. Add small stripes between red felt using red permanent marker.

8. Sew 2 thicknesses of monofilament thread to the top of the small ornaments. String white, gold and red wooden beads onto thread. Sew hanging ornaments to edge of cuff.

STOCKING WITH ATTACHED ORNAMENTS

FABRIC REQUIREMENTS
Yardage is based on 60"w felt. Felt is also available in 9" x 12" precut pieces.
  3/8 yd (34 cm) of white felt
  3/8 yd (34 cm) of red felt
  Scraps of green and gold felt
You will also need:
  Fabric glue
  10 red 3/8" (10 mm) buttons
  10 white 3/8" (10 mm) buttons
  2 white 5/8" (16 mm) buttons
  Green embroidery floss

CUTTING OUT THE PIECES
Patterns are on pages 78-81.
1. From white felt:
   • Cut 1 stocking using outer line
   • Cut 2 large candy canes
   • Cut 2 large peppermints.
   • Cut 2 stocking cuffs.
   • Cut 2 strips 1/2" x 6" using pinking shears.
2. From red felt:
   • Cut 1 stocking using inner line.
   • Cut 1 strip 5/8" x 9" for hanger.
   • Cut 7 large candy cane stripes.
   • Cut 4 large peppermint stripes.
3. From green felt:
   • Cut 1 toe
   • Cut 1 heel.
   • Cut 3 large pointed leaves.
   • Cut 2 large rounded leaves.
4. From gold felt:
   • Cut 4 large stars.
   • Cut 1 large peppermint center.
   • Cut 1 flower center.

MAKING THE STOCKING
Refer to photo, page 67, for placement of pieces.
1. Follow instructions on pages 72-73 to make 2 **Star Ornaments** (omitting tassels), 1 **Candy Cane Ornament**, 1 **Flower Ornament**, and 1 **Peppermint Ornament**.
2. Using green thread, sew toe and heel to red stocking. Sew pinked white strips over inside edges of toe and heel; trim ends of strips.
3. Sew 4 small white buttons to heel and 6 small white buttons to toe.

4. Center red stocking on white stocking; leaving top edge open, sew stockings together 1/4" from edge. Pink white stocking 1/8" from red stocking.
5. Center and sew 8 red buttons in scallops across 1 stocking cuff using black thread. Stitch 3 Lazy Daisy leaves around each button using 2 strands of green floss.
6. Sew stocking cuffs together at each side using 1/4" seam. Leave wrong side out and place inside stocking, lining up tops. Fold hanger in half and place between stocking and cuff, lining up ends of hanger with top of stocking. Sew cuff to stocking, catching both ends of hanger in seam. Turn cuff to outside.
7. Glue ornaments in place using fabric glue.

FLOWER ORNAMENT

FABRIC REQUIREMENTS
For each ornament:
  Scrap of red felt
  Scrap of gold felt
  Scrap of green
You will also need:
  Fabric glue
  Scrap of fleece

CUTTING OUT THE PIECES
Patterns are on page 81.
1. From red felt:
   • Cut 2 flowers.
2. From gold felt:
   • Cut 1 flower center.
3. From green felt:
   • Cut 3 large pointed leaves.
4. From fleece:
   • Cut 1 flower.

MAKING THE ORNAMENT
Refer to photo, page 69, for placement of pieces. Use a 1/4" seam allowance for all sewing.
1. Glue flower center to 1 flower. Satin Stitch along detail lines and around flower center as shown on pattern.
2. With right sides together, layer flower back, front and fleece. Stitch completely around flower; clip curves.
3. To turn, cut slit in center back of flower. Turn flower to right side; whipstitch opening closed.
4. Satin Stitch center veins in each leaf. Glue or tack leaves to back of flower.

STAR ORNAMENT

FABRIC REQUIREMENTS

For each ornament:
> Scrap of gold felt

You will also need:
> 1 white ⅝" (16 mm) button
> 1 red ⅜" (10 mm) button
> 1 gold wooden bead
> Red embroidery floss
> Scrap of fleece

CUTTING OUT THE PIECES

Pattern is on page 81.
1. From gold felt:
   - Cut 2 large stars.
2. From fleece:
   - Cut 1 large star.

MAKING THE ORNAMENT

Refer to photo, page 69, for placement of pieces. Use a ¼" seam allowance for all sewing.
1. Layer star front, back, and batting. Stitch completely around star; clip angles and points.
2. To turn, cut slit in center of back of star. Turn star to right side; whipstitch opening closed.
3. Center buttons on front of star, and attach with white thread, sewing through both buttons.
4. Follow **Making a Tassel**, page 96, to make tassel from red embroidery floss, running tassel ties through gold bead with embroidery needle. Run tassel ties between layers of star and out back at center of star; tie off.

PEPPERMINT ORNAMENT

FABRIC REQUIREMENTS

For each ornament:
> Scrap of white felt
> Scrap of red felt
> Scrap of gold felt
> Scrap of green felt

You will also need:
> Fabric glue
> Scrap of fleece

CUTTING OUT THE PIECES

Patterns are on page 75.
1. From white felt:
   - Cut 2 large peppermints.
2. From red felt:
   - Cut 4 large peppermint stripes.
3. From gold felt:
   - Cut 1 large peppermint center.
4. From green felt:
   - Cut 2 large rounded leaves.
5. From fleece:
   - Cut 1 large peppermint.

MAKING THE ORNAMENT

Refer to photo for placement of pieces. Use a ¼" seam allowance for all sewing.
1. Sew stripes to 1 peppermint. Machine stitch 2 lines in each white area using red thread.
2. Stitch peppermint center to striped peppermint.
3. With right sides together, layer peppermint back, front and fleece. Stitch completely around peppermint; clip curves
4. To turn, cut slit in center of back of peppermint. Turn to right side; whipstitch opening closed.
5. Cut each leaf in center and overlap ends slightly to make pucker. Glue or tack leaves to back of flower.

CANDY CANE ORNAMENT

FABRIC REQUIREMENTS

For each ornament:
> Scrap of white felt
> Scrap of red felt

You will also need:
> Fabric glue
> Scrap of fleece

CUTTING OUT THE PIECES

Patterns are on page 81.
1. From white felt:
   - Cut 2 large candy canes.
2. From red felt:
   - Cut 7 large candy cane stripes.
3. From fleece:
   - Cut 1 large candy cane.

MAKING THE ORNAMENT

Refer to photo, page 69, for placement of pieces. Use a ¼" seam allowance for all sewing.
1. Sew stripes to 1 white candy cane. Machine stitch 2 lines in each white area using red thread.
2. With right sides together, layer candy cane back, front and fleece. Stitch completely around candy cane; clip curves.
3. To turn, cut slit in center back of candy cane. Turn candy cane to right side; whipstitch opening closed.

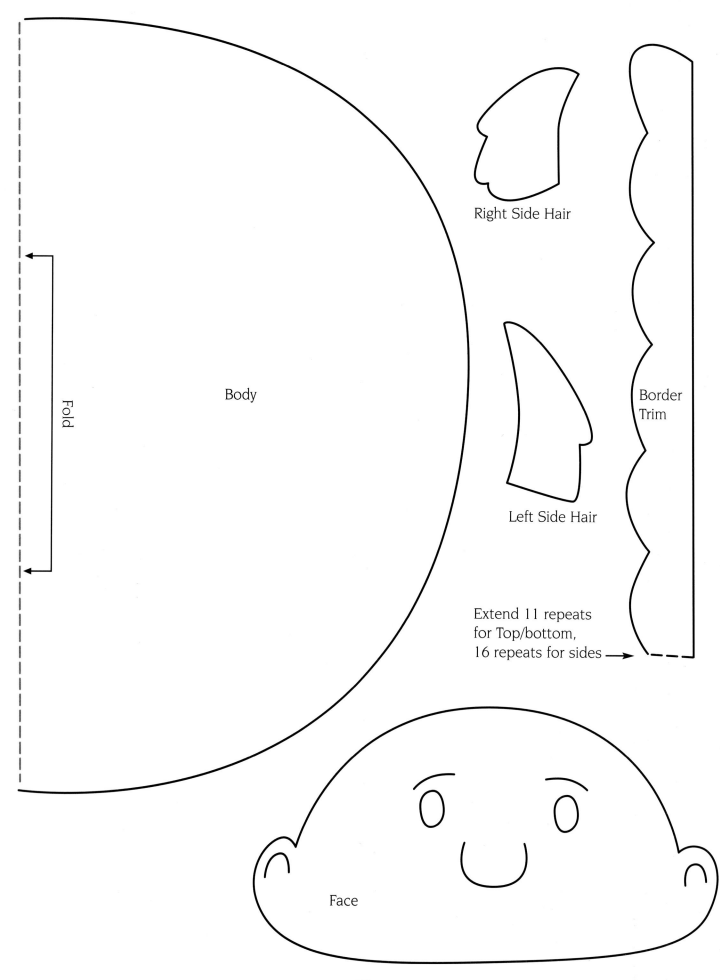

Right Side Hair

Border
Trim

Fold

Body

Left Side Hair

Extend 11 repeats
for Top/bottom,
16 repeats for sides →

Face

74

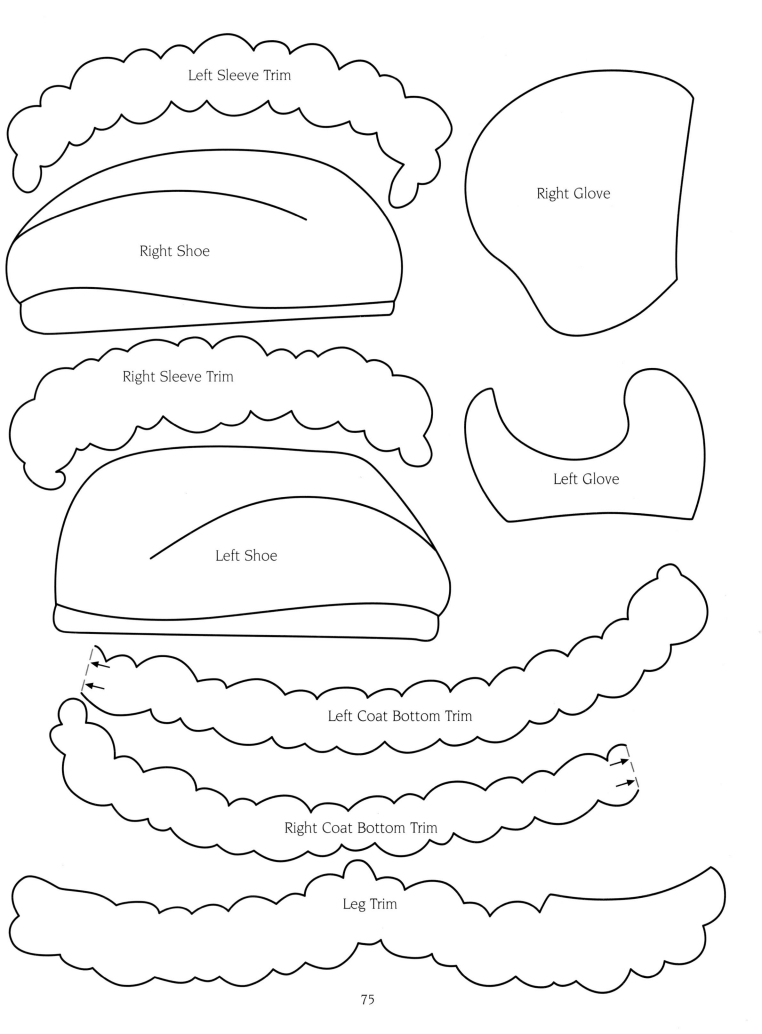

Left Sleeve Trim

Right Glove

Right Shoe

Right Sleeve Trim

Left Glove

Left Shoe

Left Coat Bottom Trim

Right Coat Bottom Trim

Leg Trim

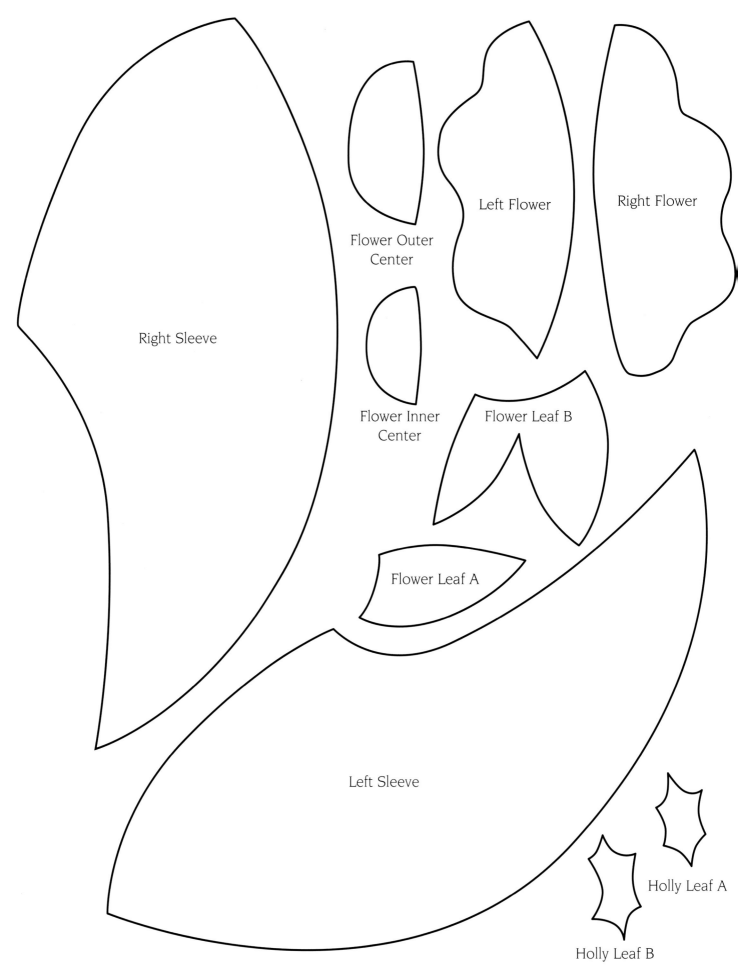

Right Sleeve

Flower Outer Center

Left Flower

Right Flower

Flower Inner Center

Flower Leaf B

Flower Leaf A

Left Sleeve

Holly Leaf A

Holly Leaf B

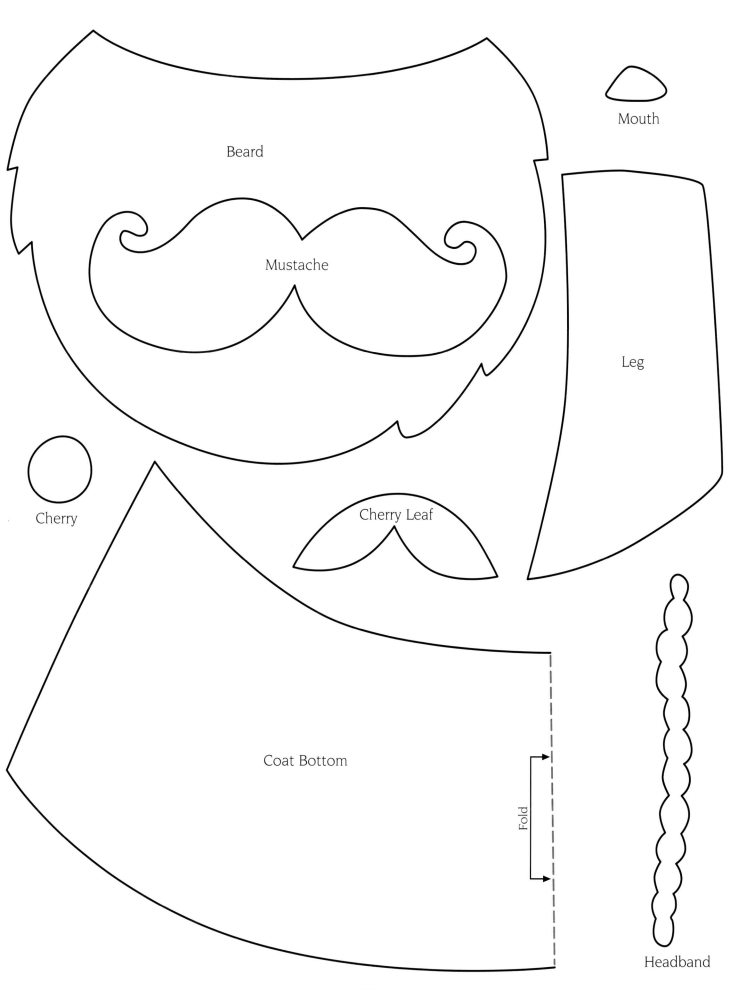

Beard

Mustache

Mouth

Leg

Cherry

Cherry Leaf

Coat Bottom

Fold

Headband

77

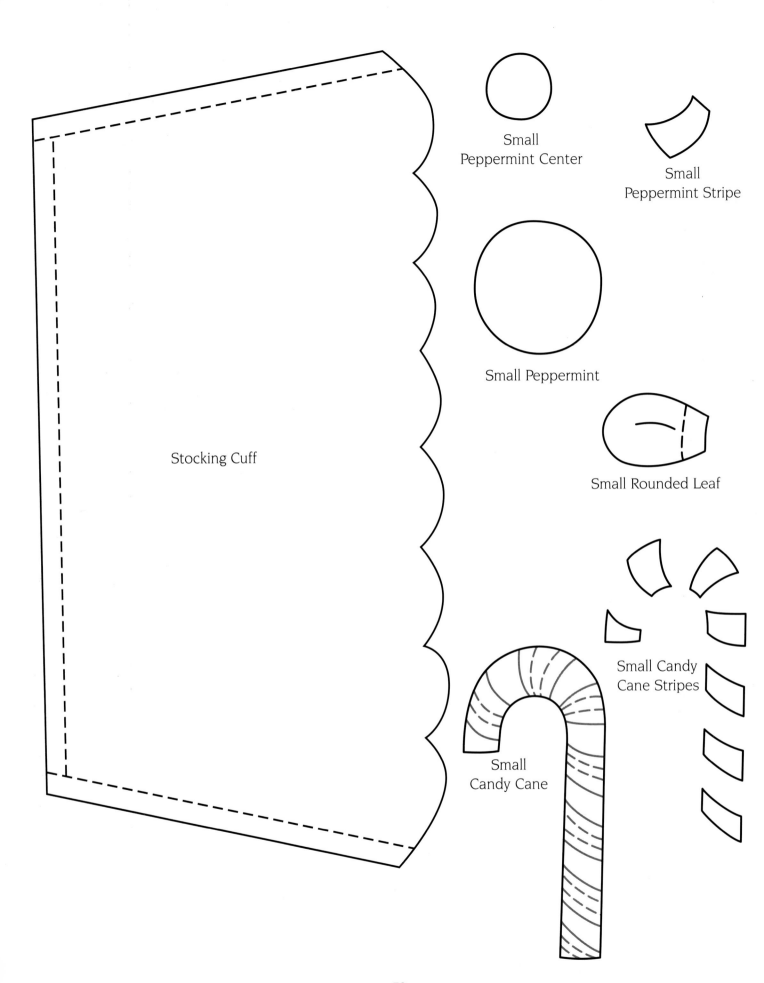

Stocking Cuff

Small Peppermint Center

Small Peppermint Stripe

Small Peppermint

Small Rounded Leaf

Small Candy Cane Stripes

Small Candy Cane

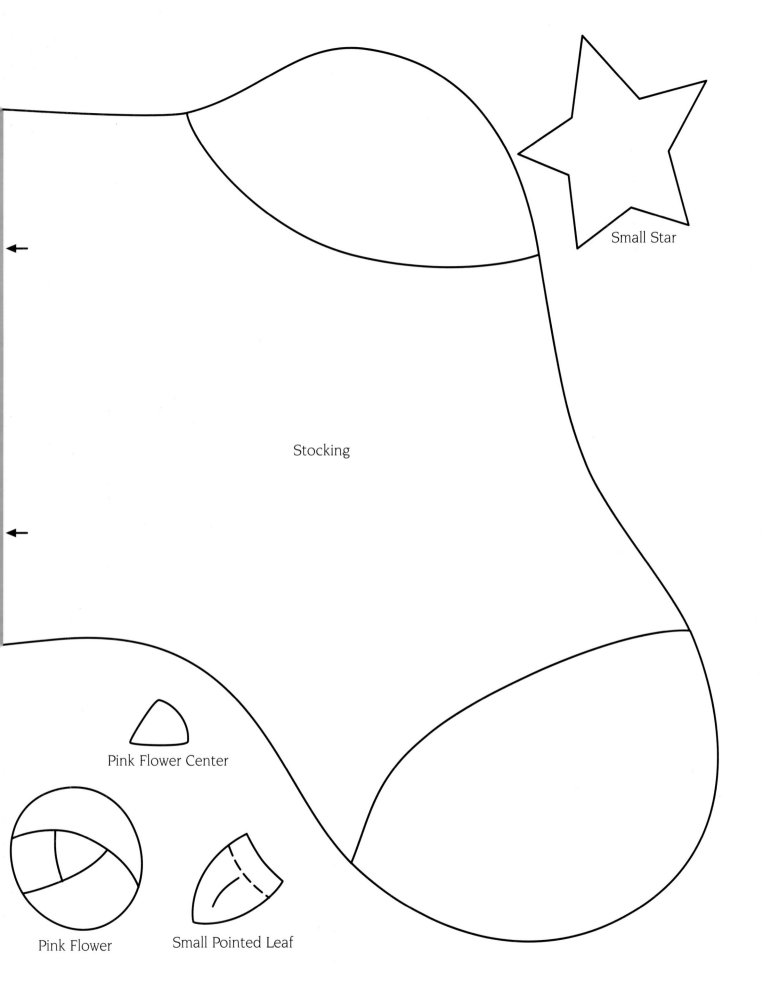

Small Star

Stocking

Pink Flower Center

Pink Flower

Small Pointed Leaf

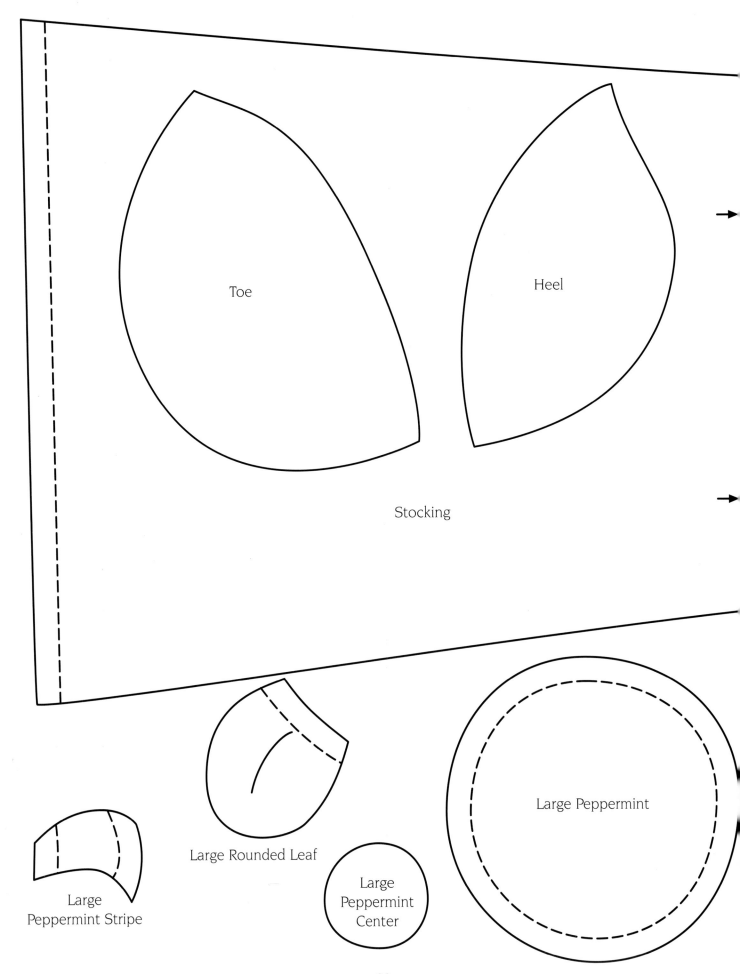

Toe

Heel

Stocking

Large Rounded Leaf

Large Peppermint

Large Peppermint Stripe

Large Peppermint Center

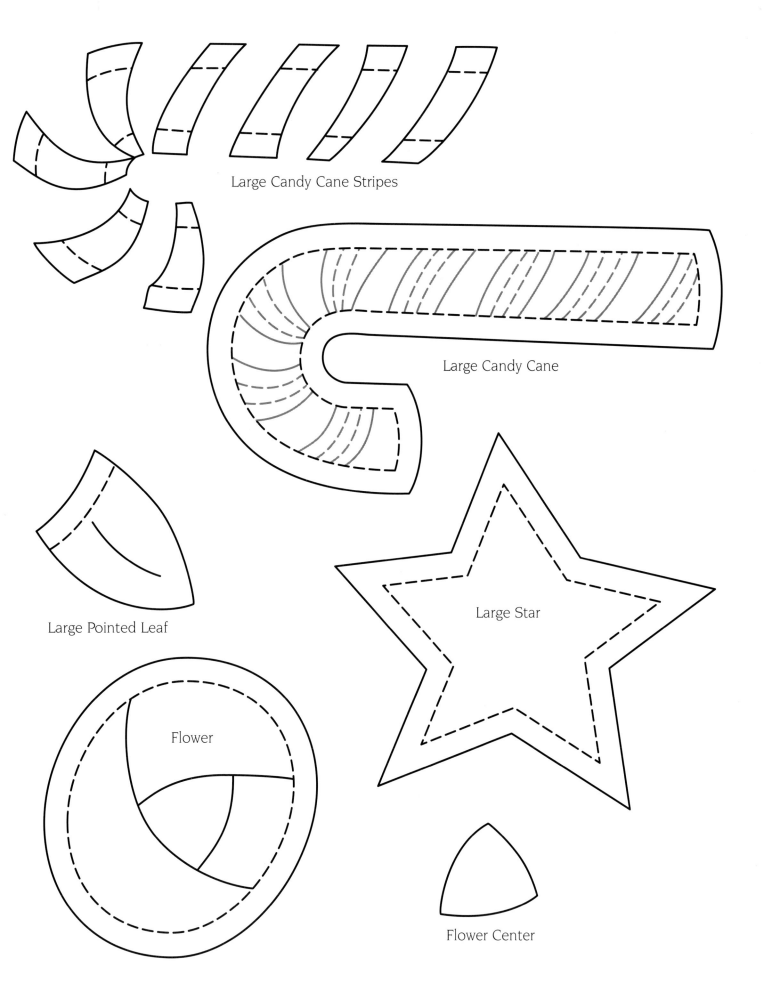

Large Candy Cane Stripes

Large Candy Cane

Large Pointed Leaf

Large Star

Flower

Flower Center

GENERAL INSTRUCTIONS

Complete instructions are given for making each of the projects shown in this book. To make your project easier and more enjoyable, we encourage you to carefully read all of the general instructions, study the color photographs, and familiarize yourself with the individual project instructions before beginning a project.

QUILTING SUPPLIES

This list includes all the tools you need for basic quiltmaking, plus additional supplies used for special techniques. Unless otherwise specified, all items may be found in your favorite fabric store or quilt shop.

Batting — Batting is most commonly available in polyester, cotton, or a polyester/cotton blend (see **Choosing and Preparing the Batting**, page 89).

Cutting mat — A cutting mat is a special mat designed to be used with a rotary cutter. A mat that measures approximately 18" X 24" is a good size for most cutting.

Eraser — A soft white fabric eraser or white art eraser may be used to remove pencil marks from fabric. Do not use a colored eraser, as the dye may discolor fabric.

Freezer paper — This heavy, white paper with a wax coating on one side will adhere temporarily to fabric when pressed on with a dry iron.

Iron — An iron with both steam and dry settings and a smooth, clean soleplate is necessary for proper pressing.

Marking tools — There are many different marking tools available (see **Marking Quilting Lines**, page 89). A silver quilter's pencil is a good marker for both light and dark fabrics.

Masking tape — Two widths of masking tape, 1"w and 1/4"w, are helpful when quilting. The 1"w tape is used to secure the backing fabric to a flat surface when layering the quilt. The 1/4"w tape may be used as a guide when outline quilting.

Needles — Two types of needles are used for hand sewing: Betweens, used for quilting, are short and strong for stitching through layered fabric and batting. Sharps are longer, thinner needles used for basting and other hand sewing. For sewing machine needles, we recommend size 10 to 14 or 70 to 90 universal (sharp-pointed) needles.

Permanent fine-point pen — A permanent pen is used to mark templates and stencils and to sign and date quilts. Test pen on fabric to make sure it will not bleed or wash out.

Pins — Straight pins made especially for quilting are extra long with large round heads. Glass head pins will stand up to occasional contact with a hot iron. Some quilters prefer extra-fine dressmaker's silk pins. If you are machine quilting, you will need a large supply of 1" long (size 01) rustproof safety pins for pin-basting.

Quilting hoop or frame — Quilting hoops and frames are designed to hold the 3 layers of a quilt together securely while you quilt. Many different types and sizes are available, including round and oval wooden hoops, frames made of rigid plastic pipe, and large floor frames made of either material. A 14" or 16" hoop allows you to quilt in your lap and makes your quilting portable.

Rotary cutter — The rotary cutter is the essential tool for quick-method quilting techniques. The cutter consists of a round, sharp blade mounted on a handle with a retractable blade guard for safety. It should be used only with a cutting mat and rotary cutting ruler. Two sizes are generally available; we recommend the larger (45 mm) size.

Rotary cutting ruler — A rotary cutting ruler is a thick, clear acrylic ruler made specifically for use with a rotary cutter. It should have accurate 1/8" crosswise and lengthwise markings and markings for 45° and 60° angles. A 6" X 24" ruler is a good size for most cutting. An additional 6" X 12" ruler or 12 1/2" square ruler is helpful when cutting wider pieces. Many specialty rulers are available that make specific cutting tasks faster and easier.

Scissors — Although most fabric cutting will be done with a rotary cutter, sharp, high-quality scissors are still needed for some cutting. A separate pair of scissors for cutting paper and plastic is recommended. Smaller scissors are handy for clipping threads.

Seam ripper — A good seam ripper with a fine point is useful for removing stitching.

Sewing machine — A sewing machine that produces a good, even straight stitch is all that is necessary for most quilting. Clean and oil your machine often and keep the tension set properly.

Tape measure — A flexible 120" long tape measure is helpful for measuring a quilt top before adding borders.

Template material — Sheets of translucent plastic, often pre-marked with a grid, are made especially for making quilting stencils.

Thimble — A thimble is necessary when hand quilting. Thimbles are available in metal, plastic, or leather and in many sizes and styles. Choose a thimble that fits well and is comfortable.

Thread — Several types of thread are used for quiltmaking: *General-purpose* sewing thread is used for basting and piecing. Choose high-quality cotton or cotton-covered polyester thread in light and dark neutrals, such as ecru and grey, for your basic supplies. *Quilting* thread is stronger than general-purpose sewing thread, and some brands have a coating to make them slide more easily through the quilt layers.

Triangle — A large plastic right-angle triangle (available in art and office supply stores) is useful in rotary cutting for making first cuts to "square up" raw edges of fabric and for checking to see that cuts remain at right angles to the fold.

Walking foot — A walking foot, or even-feed foot, is needed for straight-line machine quilting. This special foot will help all 3 layers move at the same rate over the feed dogs to provide a smoother quilted project.

FABRICS

SELECTING FABRICS

Choose high-quality, medium-weight 100% cotton fabrics such as broadcloth or calico. All-cotton fabrics hold a crease better, fray less, and are easier to quilt than cotton/polyester blends. All the fabrics for a quilt should be of comparable weight and weave. Check the end of the fabric bolt for fiber content and width.

The yardage requirements listed for most projects are based on 45" wide fabric with a "usable" width of 42" after shrinkage and trimming selvages. Your actual usable width will probably vary slightly from fabric to fabric. Though most fabrics will yield 42" or more, if you find a fabric that you suspect will yield a narrower usable width, you will need to purchase additional yardage to compensate. Our recommended yardage lengths should be adequate for occasional resquaring of fabric when many cuts are required, but it never hurts to buy a little more fabric for insurance against a narrower usable width, the occasional cutting error, or to have on hand for making coordinating projects.

PREPARING FABRICS

All fabrics should be washed, dried, and pressed before cutting.

1. To check colorfastness before washing, cut a small piece of the fabric and place in a glass of hot water with a little detergent. Leave fabric in the water for a few minutes. Remove fabric from water and blot with white paper towels. If any color bleeds onto the towels, wash the fabric separately with warm water and detergent, then rinse until the water runs clear. If fabric continues to bleed, choose another fabric.

2. Unfold yardage and separate fabrics by color. To help reduce raveling, use scissors to snip a small triangle from each corner of your fabric pieces. Machine wash fabrics in warm water with a small amount of mild laundry detergent. Do not use fabric softener. Rinse well and then dry fabrics in the dryer, checking long fabric lengths occasionally to make sure they are not tangling.

3. To make ironing easier, remove fabrics from dryer while they are slightly damp. Refold each fabric lengthwise (as it was on the bolt) with wrong sides together and matching selvages. If necessary, adjust slightly at selvages so that fold lays flat. Press each fabric using a steam iron set on "Cotton."

ROTARY CUTTING

*Based on the idea that you can easily cut strips of fabric and then cut those strips into smaller pieces, rotary cutting has brought speed and accuracy to quiltmaking. Observe safety precautions when using the rotary cutter, since it is extremely sharp. Develop a habit of retracting the blade guard **just** before making a cut and closing it **immediately afterward**, before laying down the cutter.*

1. Follow **Preparing Fabrics**, to wash, dry, and press fabrics.

2. Cut all strips from the selvage-to-selvage width of the fabric unless otherwise indicated in project instructions. Place fabric on the cutting mat, as shown in **Fig. 1**, with the fold of the fabric toward you. To straighten the uneven fabric edge, make the first "squaring up" cut by placing the right edge of the rotary cutting ruler over the left raw edge of the fabric. Place right-angle triangle (or another rotary cutting ruler) with the lower edge carefully aligned with the fold and the left edge against the ruler (**Fig. 1**). Hold the ruler firmly with your left hand, placing your little finger off the left edge to anchor the ruler. Remove the triangle, pick up the rotary cutter, and retract the blade guard. Using a smooth downward motion, make the cut by running the blade of the rotary cutter firmly along the right edge of the ruler (**Fig. 2**). **Always** cut in a direction away from your body and **immediately** close the blade guard after each cut.

Fig. 1

Fig. 2

3. To cut each of the strips required for a project, place the ruler over the cut edge of the fabric, aligning desired marking on the ruler with the cut edge (**Fig. 3**); make the cut. When cutting several strips from a single piece of fabric, it is important to occasionally use the ruler and triangle to ensure that cuts are still at a perfect right angle to the fold. If not, repeat Step 2 to straighten.

Fig. 3

4. To square up selvage ends of a strip before cutting pieces, refer to **Fig. 4** and place folded strip on mat with selvage ends to your right. Aligning a horizontal marking on ruler with 1 long edge of strip, use rotary cutter to trim selvage to make end of strip square and even (**Fig. 4**). Turn strip (or entire mat) so that cut end is to your left before making subsequent cuts.

Fig. 4

5. Pieces such as rectangles and squares can now be cut from strips. Usually strips remain folded, and pieces are cut in pairs after ends of strips are squared up. To cut squares or rectangles from a strip, place ruler over left end of strip, aligning desired marking on ruler with cut end of strip. To ensure perfectly square cuts, align a horizontal marking on ruler with 1 long edge of strip (**Fig. 5**) before making the cut.

Fig. 5

6. To cut 2 triangles from a square, cut square the size indicated in the project instructions. Cut square once diagonally to make 2 triangles (**Fig. 6**).

Fig. 6

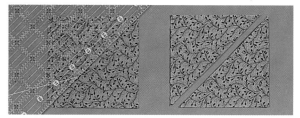

7. To cut 4 triangles from a square, cut square the size indicated in the project instructions. Cut square twice diagonally to make 4 triangles (**Fig. 7**). You may find it helpful to use a small rotary cutting mat so that the mat can be turned to make second cut without disturbing fabric pieces.

8. After some practice, you may want to try stacking up to 6 fabric layers when making cuts. When stacking strips, match long cut edges and follow Step 4 to square up ends of strip stack. Carefully turn stack (or entire mat) so that squared-up ends are to your left before making subsequent cuts. After cutting, check accuracy of pieces. Some shapes, such as diamonds, are more difficult to cut accurately in stacks.

9. In some cases, strips will be sewn together into strip sets before being cut into smaller units. When cutting a strip set, align a seam in strip set with a horizontal marking on the ruler to maintain square cuts (**Fig. 8**). We do not recommend stacking strip sets for rotary cutting.

10. Most borders for quilts in this book are cut along the more stable lengthwise grain to minimize wavy edges caused by stretching. To remove selvages before cutting lengthwise strips, place fabric on mat with selvages to your left and squared-up end at bottom of mat. Placing ruler over selvage and using squared-up edge instead of fold, follow Step 2 to cut away selvages as you did raw edges (**Fig. 9**). After making a cut the length of the mat, move the next section of fabric to be cut onto the mat. Repeat until you have removed selvages from required length of fabric.

Fig. 9

11. After removing selvages, place ruler over left edge of fabric, aligning desired marking on ruler with cut edge of fabric. Make cuts as in Step 3. After each cut, move next section of fabric onto mat as in Step 10.

PIECING AND PRESSING
Precise cutting, followed by accurate piecing and careful pressing, will ensure that all the pieces of your quilt top fit together well.

PIECING
Set sewing machine stitch length for approximately 11 stitches per inch. Use a new, sharp needle suited for medium-weight woven fabric.

Use a neutral-colored general-purpose sewing thread (not quilting thread) in the needle and in the bobbin. Stitch first on a scrap of fabric to check upper and bobbin thread tension; make any adjustments necessary.

For good results, it is **essential** that you stitch with an **accurate ¼" seam allowance**. On many sewing machines, the measurement from the needle to the outer edge of the presser foot is ¼". If this is the case with your machine, the presser foot is your best guide. If not, measure ¼" from the needle and mark throat plate with a piece of masking tape. Special presser feet that are exactly ¼" wide are also available for most sewing machines. When piecing, always place pieces right sides together and match

raw edges; pin if necessary. (If using straight pins, remove the pins just before they reach the sewing machine needle.)

Making Triangle-Squares
The grid method for making triangle-squares is faster and more accurate than cutting and sewing individual triangles. Stitching before cutting the triangle-squares apart also prevents stretching the bias edges.

1. Follow project instructions to cut rectangles or squares of fabric for making triangle-squares. Place the indicated pieces right sides together and press.
2. On the wrong side of the lighter fabric, draw a grid of squares similar to that shown in **Fig. 10**. The size and number of squares are given in the project instructions.

Fig. 10

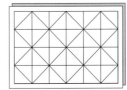

3. Following the example given in the project instructions, draw 1 diagonal line through each square in the grid (**Fig. 11**).

Fig. 11

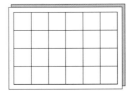

4. Stitch ¼" on each side of all diagonal lines. For accuracy, it may be helpful to first draw your stitching lines onto the fabric, especially if your presser foot is not your ¼" guide. In some cases, stitching may be done in a single continuous line. Project instructions include a diagram similar to **Fig. 12**, which shows stitching lines and the direction of the stitching.

Fig. 12

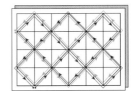

5. Use rotary cutter and ruler to cut along all drawn lines of the grid. Each square of the grid will yield 2 triangle-squares (**Fig. 13**).

Fig. 13

6. Carefully press triangle-squares open, pressing seam allowances toward darker fabric.

Chain Piecing

Chain piecing whenever possible will make your work go faster and will usually result in more accurate piecing. Stack the pieces you will be sewing beside your machine in the order you will need them and in a position that will allow you to easily pick them up. Pick up each pair of pieces, carefully place them together as they will be sewn, and feed them into the machine one after the other. Stop between each pair only long enough to pick up the next and don't cut thread between pairs (**Fig. 14**). After all pieces are sewn, cut threads, press, and go on to the next step, again chain piecing when possible.

Fig. 14

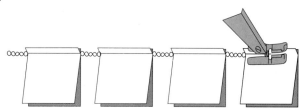

Sewing Across Seam Intersections

When sewing across the intersection of 2 seams, place pieces right sides together and match seams exactly, making sure seam allowances are pressed in opposite directions (**Fig. 15**). To prevent fabric from shifting, you may wish to pin in place.

Fig. 15

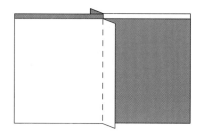

Sewing Bias Seams

Care should be used in handling and stitching bias edges since they stretch easily. After sewing the seam, carefully press seam allowance to 1 side, making sure not to stretch fabric.

Sewing Sharp Points

To ensure sharp points when joining triangular or diagonal pieces, stitch across the center of the "X" (shown in pink) formed on the wrong side by previous seams (**Fig. 16**).

Fig. 16

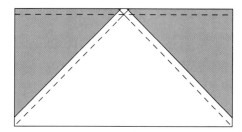

Trimming Seam Allowances

When sewing with triangle pieces, some seam allowances may extend beyond the edges of the sewn pieces. Trim away "dog ears" that extend beyond the edges of the sewn pieces (**Fig. 17**).

Fig. 17

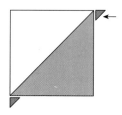

PRESSING

Use a steam iron set on "Cotton" for all pressing. Press as you sew, taking care to prevent small folds along seamlines. Seam allowances are almost always pressed to one side, usually toward the darker fabric. However, to reduce bulk it may occasionally be necessary to press seam allowances toward the lighter fabric or even to press them open. In order to prevent a dark fabric seam allowance from showing through a light fabric, trim the darker seam allowance slightly narrower than the lighter seam allowance. To press long seams, such as those in long strip sets, without curving or other distortion, lay strips across the width of the ironing board.

APPLIQUÉ

PREPARING FUSIBLE APPLIQUÉS

Patterns for fused appliqués are printed in reverse to enable you to use our speedy method of preparing appliqués. White or light-colored fabrics may need to be lined with fusible interfacing before applying fusible web to prevent darker fabrics from showing through.

1. Place paper-backed fusible web, web side down, over appliqué pattern. Use a pencil to trace pattern onto paper side of web as many times as indicated in project instructions for a single fabric. Repeat for additional patterns and fabrics.

2. Follow manufacturers instructions to fuse traced patterns to wrong side of fabrics. Do not remove paper backing. (Note: Some pieces may be given as measurements, such as a 2" x 4" rectangle, instead of drawn patterns. Fuse web to wrong side of the fabrics indicated for these pieces.)

3. Use scissors to cut out appliqué pieces along traced lines; use rotary cutting equipment to cut out appliqué pieces given as measurements. Remove paper backing from all pieces.

SATIN STITCH APPLIQUÉ

A good satin stitch is a thick, smooth, almost solid line of zigzag stitching that covers the exposed raw edges of appliqué pieces.

1. Place a stabilizer, such as paper or any of the commercially available products, on wrong side of background fabric before stitching appliqués in place.

2. Thread needle of sewing machine with general-purpose thread. Use thread that matches the background fabric in the bobbin for all stitching. Set sewing machine for a medium width zigzag stitch (approximately 1/8") and a very short stitch length. Set upper tension slightly looser than for regular stitching.

3. Beginning on as straight an edge as possible, position fabric so that most of the satin stitch will be on the appliqué piece. Do not backstitch; hold upper thread toward you and sew over it two or three stitches to anchor thread. Following Steps 4–7 for stitching corners and curves, stitch over exposed raw edges of appliqué pieces, changing thread color as necessary.

4. (Note: Dots on **Figs. 18 - 23** indicate where to leave needle in fabric when pivoting.) For **outside corners**, stitch just past the corner, stopping with the needle in **background** fabric (**Fig. 18**). Raise presser foot. Pivot project, lower presser foot, and stitch adjacent side (**Fig. 19**).

Fig. 18   Fig. 19

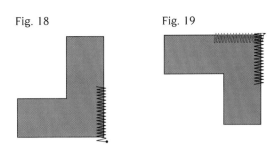

5. For **inside corners**, stitch just past the corner, stopping with the needle in **appliqué** fabric (**Fig. 20**). Raise presser foot. Pivot project, lower presser foot, and stitch adjacent side (**Fig. 21**).

Fig. 20   Fig. 21

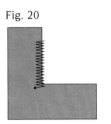 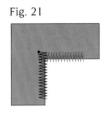

6. When stitching **outside** curves, stop with needle in **background** fabric. Raise presser foot and pivot project as needed. Lower presser foot and continue stitching, pivoting as often as necessary to follow curve (**Fig. 22**).

Fig. 22

7. When stitching **inside** curves, stop with needle in **appliqué** fabric. Raise presser foot and pivot project as needed. Lower presser foot and continue stitching, pivoting as often as necessary to follow curve (**Fig. 23**).

Fig. 23

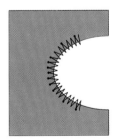

8. Do not backstitch at end of stitching. Pull threads to wrong side of background fabric; knot thread and trim ends. Remove paper and stabilizer.

INVISIBLE APPLIQUÉ

This machine appliqué method uses clear nylon thread to secure the appliqué pieces. Transparent monofilament (clear nylon) thread is available in 2 colors: clear and smoke. Use clear on white or very light fabrics and smoke on darker colors.

1. Thread sewing machine with transparent monofilament thread; use general-purpose thread that matches background fabric in bobbin.
2. Set sewing machine for a very narrow (approximately 1/16") zigzag stitch and a short stitch length. You may find that loosening the top tension slightly will yield a smoother stitch.
3. To stitch appliqués, follow steps **3-8** of **Satin Stitch Appliqué**.

BORDERS

Borders cut along the lengthwise grain will lie flatter than borders cut along the crosswise grain. Cutting lengths given for most borders in this book are exact. You may wish to add an extra 2" of length at each end for "insurance"; borders will be trimmed after measuring completed center section of quilt top.

1. Mark the center of each edge of quilt top.
2. Most of the borders in this book have the side borders added first. To add side borders, measure across center of quilt top to determine length of borders (**Fig. 24**). Trim side borders to the determined length.

Fig. 24

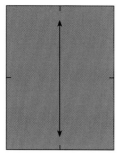

3. Mark center of 1 long edge of side border. Matching center marks and raw edges, pin border to quilt top, easing in any fullness; stitch. Repeat for other side border.

4. Measure center of quilt top, including attached borders, to determine length of top and bottom borders. Trim top and bottom borders to the determined length. Repeat Step 3 to add borders to quilt top (**Fig. 25**).

Fig. 25

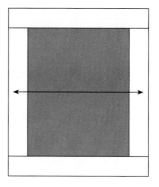

QUILTING

*Quilting holds the 3 layers (top, batting, and backing) of the quilt together and can be done by hand or machine. Our project instructions tell you which method is used on each project and show you quilting diagrams that can be used as suggestions for marking quilting designs. Because marking, layering, and quilting are interrelated and may be done in different orders depending on circumstances, please read the entire **Quilting** section, pages 88 - 91, before beginning the quilting process on your project.*

TYPES OF QUILTING
In the Ditch

Quilting very close to a seamline or appliqué is called "in the ditch" quilting. This type of quilting does not need to be marked. When quilting in the ditch, quilt on the side opposite the seam allowance.

Outline Quilting

Quilting approximately 1/4" from a seam or appliqué is called "outline" quilting. Outline quilting may be marked, or you may place 1/4"w masking tape along seamlines and quilt along the opposite edge of the tape. (Do not leave tape on quilt longer than necessary, since it may leave an adhesive residue.)

MARKING QUILTING LINES

Fabric marking pencils, various types of chalk markers, and fabric marking pens with inks that disappear with exposure to air or water are readily available and work well for different applications. Lead pencils work well on light-color fabrics, but marks may be difficult to remove. White pencils work well on dark-color fabrics, and silver pencils show up well on many colors. Since chalk rubs off easily, it's a good choice if you are marking as you quilt. Fabric marking pens make more durable and visible markings, but the marks should be carefully removed according to manufacturer's instructions. Press down only as hard as necessary to make a visible line.

When you choose to mark your quilt, whether before or after the layers are basted together, is also a factor in deciding which marking tool to use. If you mark with chalk or a chalk pencil, handling the quilt during basting may rub off the markings. Intricate or ornamental designs may not be practical to mark as you quilt; mark these designs before basting using a more durable marker.

To choose marking tools, take all these factors into consideration and test different markers on scrap fabric until you find the one that gives the desired result.

USING QUILTING STENCILS

A wide variety of precut quilting stencils, as well as entire books of quilting patterns, are available. Using a stencil makes it easier to mark intricate or repetitive designs on your quilt top.

1. To make a stencil from a pattern, center template plastic over pattern and use a permanent marker to trace pattern onto plastic.
2. Use a craft knife with a single or double blade to cut narrow slits along traced lines (**Fig. 26**).

Fig. 26

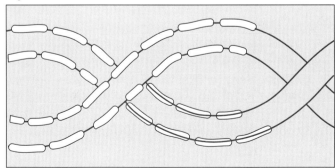

3. Use desired marking tool and stencil to mark quilting lines.

CHOOSING AND PREPARING THE BACKING

To allow for slight shifting of the quilt top during quilting, the backing should be approximately 4" larger on all sides or a bed-size quilt top or approximately 2" larger on all sides for a wall hanging. Yardage requirements listed for quilt backings are calculated for 45"w fabric. If you are making a bed-size quilt, using 90"w or 108"w fabric for the backing may eliminate piecing. To piece a backing using 45"w fabric, use the following instructions.

1. Measure length and width of quilt top; add 8" (4" for a wall hanging) to each measurement.
2. If quilt top is 76"w or less, cut backing fabric into 2 lengths slightly longer than the determined length measurement. Trim selvages. Place lengths with right sides facing and sew long edges together, forming a tube (**Fig. 27**). Match seams and press along 1 fold (**Fig. 28**). Cut along pressed fold to form a single piece (**Fig. 29**).

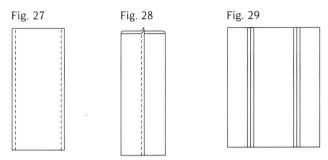

Fig. 27   Fig. 28   Fig. 29

3. If quilt top is more than 76"w, cut backing fabric into 3 lengths slightly longer than the determined width measurement. Trim selvages. Sew long edges together to form a single piece.

4. Trim backing to correct size, if necessary, and press seam allowances open.

CHOOSING AND PREPARING THE BATTING

Choosing the right batting will make your quilting job easier. For fine hand quilting, choose a low-loft batting in any of the fiber types described here. Machine quilters will want to choose a low-loft batting that is all cotton or a cotton/polyester blend because the cotton helps "grip" the layers of the quilt. If the quilt is to be tied, a high-loft batting, sometimes called extra-loft or fat batting, is a good choice.

Batting is available in many different fibers. Bonded polyester batting is one of the most popular batting types. It is treated with a protective coating to stabilize the fibers and to reduce "bearding," a process in which batting fibers work their way out through the quilt fabrics. Other batting options include cotton/polyester batting, which combines the best of both polyester and cotton battings; all-cotton batting, which must be quilted more closely than polyester batting; and wool and silk battings, which are generally more expensive and usually only dry-cleanable.

Whichever batting you choose, read the manufacturer's instructions closely for any special notes on care or preparation. When you're ready to use your chosen batting in a project, cut batting the same size as the prepared backing.

ASSEMBLING THE QUILT

1. Examine wrong side of quilt top closely; trim any seam allowances and clip any threads that may show through the front of the quilt. Press quilt top.
2. If quilt top is to be marked before layering, mark quilting lines (see **Marking Quilting Lines**, page 89).
3. Place backing wrong side up on a flat surface. Use masking tape to tape edges of backing to surface. Place batting on top of backing fabric. Smooth batting gently, being careful not to stretch or tear. Center quilt top right side up on batting.
4. If hand quilting, begin in the center and work toward the outer edges to hand baste all layers together. Use long stitches and place basting lines approximately 4" apart (**Fig. 30**). Smooth fullness or wrinkles toward outer edges.

Fig. 30

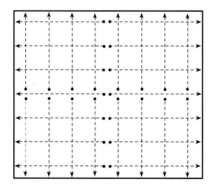

5. If machine quilting, use 1" rustproof safety pins to "pin-baste" all layers together, spacing pins approximately 4" apart. Begin at the center and work toward the outer edges to secure all layers. If possible, place pins away from areas that will be quilted, although pins may be removed as needed when quilting.

HAND QUILTING

The quilting stitch is a basic running stitch that forms a broken line on the quilt top and backing. Stitches on the quilt top and backing should be straight and equal in length.

1. Secure center of quilt in hoop or frame. Check quilt top and backing to make sure they are smooth. To help prevent puckers, always begin quilting in the center of the quilt and work toward the outside edges.
2. Thread needle with an 18"-20" length of quilting thread; knot 1 end. Using a thimble, insert needle into quilt top and batting approximately $1/2$" from where you wish to begin quilting. Bring needle up at the point where you wish to begin (**Fig. 31**); when knot catches on quilt top, give thread a quick, short pull to "pop" knot through fabric into batting (**Fig. 32**).

Fig. 31

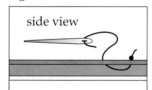

side view

Fig. 32

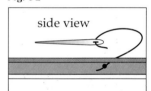

side view

3. Holding the needle with your sewing hand and placing your other hand underneath the quilt, use thimble to push the tip of the needle down through all layers. As soon as needle touches your finger underneath, use that finger to push the tip of the needle only back up through the layers to top of quilt. (The amount of the needle showing above the fabric determines the length of the quilting stitch.) Referring to **Fig. 33**, rock the needle up and down, taking 3 - 6 stitches before bringing the needle and thread completely through the layers. Check the back of the quilt to make sure stitches are going through all layers. When quilting through a seam allowance or quilting a curve or corner, you may need to make 1 stitch at a time.

Fig. 33

4. When you reach the end of your thread, knot thread close to the fabric and "pop" knot into batting; clip thread close to fabric.

5. Stop and move your hoop as often as necessary. You do not have to tie a knot every time you move your hoop; you may leave the thread dangling and pick it up again when you return to that part of the quilt.

MACHINE QUILTING

The following instructions are for straight-line quilting, which requires a walking foot or even-feed foot. The term "straight-line" is somewhat deceptive, since curves (especially gentle ones) as well as straight lines can be stitched with this technique.

1. Wind your sewing machine bobbin with general-purpose thread that matches the quilt backing. Do not use quilting thread. Thread the needle of your machine with transparent monofilament thread if you want your quilting to blend with your quilt top fabrics. Use decorative thread, such as a metallic or contrasting-color general-purpose thread, when you want the quilting lines to stand out more. Set the stitch length for 6 - 10 stitches per inch and attach the walking foot to sewing machine.

2. After pin-basting, decide which section of the quilt will have the longest continuous quilting line, oftentimes the area from center top to center bottom. Leaving the area exposed where you will place your first line of quilting, roll up each edge of the quilt to help reduce the bulk, keeping fabrics smooth. Smaller projects may not need to be rolled.

3. Start stitching at beginning of longest quilting line, using very short stitches for the first 1/4" to "lock" beginning of quilting line. Stitch across project, using one hand on each side of the walking foot to slightly spread the fabric and to guide the fabric through the machine. Lock stitches at end of quilting line.

4. Continue machine quilting, stitching longer quilting lines first to stabilize the quilt before moving on to other areas.

MACHINE STIPPLE QUILTING

The term, "stipple quilting," refers to dense quilting using a meandering line of machine stitching or closely spaced hand stitching.

1. Wind your sewing machine bobbin with general-purpose thread that matches the quilt backing. Do not use quilting thread. Thread the needle of your machine with transparent monofilament thread if you want your quilting to blend with your quilt top fabrics. Use decorative thread, such as a metallic or contrasting-colored general-purpose thread, when you want the quilting lines to stand out more.

2. For random stipple quilting, use a darning foot, drop or cover feed dogs, and set stitch length at zero. Pull up bobbin thread and hold both thread ends while you stitch 2 or 3 stitches in place to lock thread. Cut threads near quilt surface. Place hands lightly on quilt on either side of darning foot.

3. Begin stitching in a meandering pattern (**Fig. 34**), guiding the quilt with your hands. The object is to make stitches of similar length and to not sew over previous stitching lines. The movement of your hands is what determines the stitch length; it takes practice to coordinate your hand motions and the pressure you put on the foot pedal, so go slowly at first.

Fig. 34

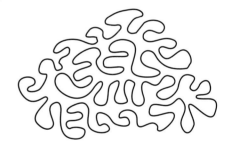

4. Continue machine quilting, filling in one open area of the quilt before moving on to another area, locking thread again at end of each line of stitching by sewing 2 or 3 stitches in place and trimming thread ends.

BINDING

Binding encloses the raw edges of your quilt. Because of its stretchiness, bias binding works well for binding projects with curves or rounded corners and tends to lie smooth and flat in any given circumstance. It is also more durable than other types of binding.

Making Continuous Bias Strip Binding

Bias strips for binding can simply be cut and pieced to the desired length. However, when a long length of binding is needed, the "continuous" method is quick and accurate.

1. Cut a square from binding fabric the size indicated in the project instructions. Cut square in half diagonally to make 2 triangles.
2. With right sides together and using a 1/4" seam allowance, sew triangles together (**Fig. 35**); press seam allowance open.

Fig. 35

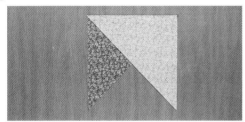

3. On wrong side of fabric, draw lines the width of the binding as specified in the project instructions, usually 2 1/2" (**Fig. 36**). Cut off any remaining fabric less than this width.

Fig. 36

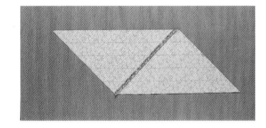

4. With right sides inside, bring short edges together to form a tube; match raw edges so that first drawn line of top section meets second drawn line of bottom section (**Fig. 37**).

Fig. 37

5. Carefully pin edges together by inserting pins through drawn lines at the point where drawn lines intersect, making sure the pins go through intersections on both sides. Using a 1/4" seam allowance, sew edges together. Press seam allowance open.

6. To cut continuous strip, begin cutting along first drawn line (**Fig. 38**). Continue cutting along drawn line around tube.

Fig. 38

7. Trim ends of bias strip square.
8. Matching wrong sides and raw edges, press bias strip in half lengthwise to complete binding.

Making Single Straight-Grain Binding

1. To determine length of strip needed for binding with mitered corners, measure the edges of the quilt and add 12".
2. Cut strips of binding fabric the width called for in the project instructions, piecing as necessary.
3. Press under one long edge 1/4", then follow **Attaching Binding With Mitered Corners**.

Attaching Binding With Mitered Corners

1. Press 1 end of binding diagonally (**Fig. 39**).

Fig. 39

2. Beginning with pressed end several inches from a corner, lay binding around quilt to make sure that seams in binding will not end up at a corner. Adjust placement if necessary. Matching raw edges of binding to raw edge of quilt top, pin binding to right side of quilt along 1 edge.
3. When you reach the first corner, mark 1/4" from corner of quilt top (**Fig. 40**).

Fig. 40

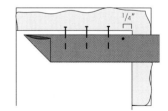

4. Using a ¼" seam allowance, sew binding to quilt, backstitching at beginning of stitching and when you reach the mark (**Fig. 41**). Lift needle out of fabric and clip thread.

Fig. 41

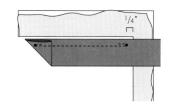

5. Fold binding as shown in **Figs. 42 and 43** and pin binding to adjacent side, matching raw edges. When you reach the next corner, mark ¼" from edge of quilt top.

Fig. 42   Fig. 43

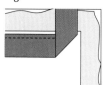

6. Backstitching at edge of quilt top, sew pinned binding to quilt (**Fig. 44**); backstitch when you reach the next mark. Lift needle out of fabric and clip thread.

Fig. 44

7. Repeat Steps 5 and 6 to continue sewing binding to quilt until binding overlaps beginning end by approximately 2". Trim excess binding.
8. If using 2½"w binding (finished size ½"), trim backing and batting a scant ¼" larger than quilt top so that batting and backing will fill the binding when it is folded over to the quilt backing. If using narrower binding, trim backing and batting even with edges of quilt top.
9. On 1 edge of quilt, fold binding over to quilt backing and pin pressed edge in place, covering stitching line (**Fig. 45**). On adjacent side, fold binding over, forming a mitered corner (**Fig. 46**). Repeat to pin remainder of binding in place.

Fig. 45   Fig. 46

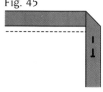   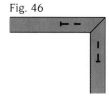

10. Blindstitch binding to backing, taking care not to stitch through to front of quilt (**Fig.47**). To make blindstitch, come up at 1. Go down at 2 and come up at 3. Length of stitches may be varied as desired.

Fig. 47

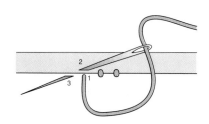

MAKING A HANGING SLEEVE

Attaching a hanging sleeve to the back of your wall hanging or quilt before the binding is added allows you to display your completed project on a wall.

1. Measure the width of the wall hanging top and subtract 1". Cut a piece of fabric 7"w by the determined measurement.
2. Press short edges of fabric piece ¼" to wrong side; press edges ¼" to wrong side again and machine stitch in place.
3. Matching wrong sides, fold piece in half lengthwise to form a tube.
4. Follow project instructions to sew binding to quilt top and to trim backing and batting. Before blindstitching binding to backing, match raw edges and stitch hanging sleeve to center top edge on back of wall hanging.
5. Finish binding wall hanging, treating the hanging sleeve as part of the backing.
6. Blindstitch bottom of hanging sleeve to backing, taking care not to stitch through to front of quilt.
7. Insert dowel or slat into hanging sleeve.

EMBROIDERY STITCHES
Backstitch
Come up at 1, go down at 2, and come up at 3 (**Fig. 48**). Continue working as shown in **Fig. 49**. Length of stitches may be varied as desired.

Fig. 48   Fig. 49

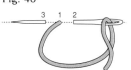   

Blanket Stitch

Come up at 1. Go down at 2 and come up at 3, keeping thread below point of needle (**Fig. 50**). Continue working as shown in **Fig. 51**.

Fig. 50

Fig. 51

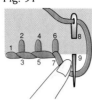

Couching Stitch

Come up at 1. Go down at 2, and up at 3. Continue unit first stitch is evenly covered by small stitches (**Fig. 52**).

Fig. 52

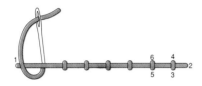

Cross Stitch

Come up at 1 and go down at 2. Come up at 3 and go down at 4. (**Fig. 53 -54**).

Fig. 53

Fig. 54

French Knot

Follow Figs. **55 –58** to complete French Knots. Come up at 1. Wrap thread twice around needle and insert needle at 2, holding end of thread with non-stitching fingers. Tighten knot; then pull needle through, holding floss until it must be released. For larger knot, use more strands; wrap only once.

Fig. 55

Fig. 56

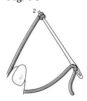

Fig. 57

Fig. 58

Lazy Daisy Stitch

Bring needle up at 1; take needle down again at 1 to form a loop and bring needle up at 2. Keeping loop below point of needle (**Fig. 59**), take needle down at 3 to anchor loop (**Fig. 60**).

Fig. 59

Fig. 60

Running Stitch

The running stitch consists of a series of straight stitches with the stitch length equal to the space between stitches (**Fig. 61**).

Fig. 61

Satin Stitch

Come up at 1. Go down at 2, and come up at 3. Continue until area is filled (**Fig. 62**).

Fig. 62

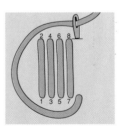

Stem Stitch

Come up at 1. Keeping thread below stitching line, go down at 2 and come up at 3. Go down at 4 and come up at 5 (**Fig. 63**).

Fig. 63

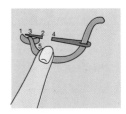

Straight Stitch

Bring needle up at 1 and take needle down at 2 (**Fig. 64**). Length of stitches may be varied as desired.

Fig. 64

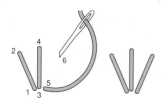

PILLOW FINISHING

If desired, you may add welting and/or a ruffle to the pillow top before sewing the pillow top and back together.

ADDING WELTING TO PILLOW TOP

1. To make welting, use bias strip indicated in project instructions. (Or measure edges of pillow top and add 4". Measure circumference of cord and add 2". Cut a bias strip of fabric the determined measurement, piecing if necessary.)
2. Lay cord along center of bias strip on wrong side of fabric; fold strip over cord. Using a zipper foot, machine baste close to cord. Trim seam allowance to the width you will use to sew pillow top and back together (see step 2 of **Making a Knife-Edge Pillow, page 96**).
3. Matching raw edges and beginning and ending 3" from ends of welting, baste welting to right side of pillow top. To make turning corners easier, clip seam allowance of welting at pillow top corners.
4. Remove approximately 3" of seam at 1 end of welting; fold fabric away from cord. Trim remaining end of welting so that cord ends meet exactly (**Fig. 65**).

Fig. 65

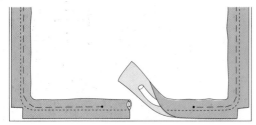

5. Fold short edge of welting fabric ¹/₂" to wrong side; fold fabric back over area where ends meet (**Fig. 66**).

Fig. 66

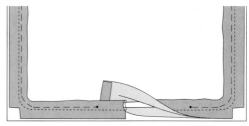

6. Baste remainder of welting to pillow top close to cord (**Fig. 67**).

Fig. 67

7. Follow **Making a Knife-Edge Pillow**, page 96, to complete pillow.

ADDING RUFFLE TO PILLOW TOP

1. To make ruffle, use fabric strip indicated in project instructions.
2. Matching right sides, use a ¹/₄" seam allowance to sew short edges of ruffle together to form a large circle; press seam allowance open. With wrong sides together and matching raw edges, fold along length of circle; press.
3. To gather ruffle, place quilting thread ¹/₄" from raw edge of ruffle. Using a medium-width zigzag stitch with medium stitch length, stitch over quilting thread, being careful not to catch quilting thread in stitching. Pull quilting thread, drawing up gathers to fit pillow top.
4. Follow **Making A Knife-Edge Pillow**, page 96, to complete pillow.

MAKING A KNIFE-EDGE PILLOW

1. For pillow back, cut a piece of fabric the same size as the pillow top.
2. Place pillow back and pillow top right sides together. The seam allowance width you will use will depend on the construction of the pillow top. If the pillow top has borders on which the finished width of the border is not crucial, use a $1/2$" seam allowance for durability. If the pillow top is pieced so that a wider seam allowance would interfere with the design, use a $1/4$" seam allowance. Using the determined seam allowance (or stitching as close as possible to the welting), sew pillow top and back together, leaving and opening at bottom edge for turning.
3. Turn pillow right side out, carefully pushing corners outward. Stuff with fiberfill or a pillow form and sew opening closed by hand.

MAKING A TASSEL

Determine desired finished length of tassel. Cut a piece of cardboard 3" wide by determined length. Using embroidery floss, follow Figs. 68-71 to make tassel.

Fig. 68

Fig. 69

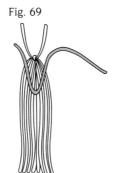

Fig. 70

Fig. 71

SIGNING AND DATING YOUR QUILT

Your completed quilt is a work of art and should be signed and dated. There are many different ways to do this, and you should pick a method that reflects the style of the quilt, the occasion for which it was made, and your own particular talents.

The following suggestions may give you an idea for recording the history of your quilt for future generations.

- Embroider your name, the date, and any additional information on the quilt top or backing. You may choose embroidery floss colors that closely match the fabric you are working on, such as white floss on a white border, or contrasting colors may be used.
- Make a label from muslin and use a permanent marker to write your information. Your label may be as plain or as fancy as you wish. Stitch the label to the back of the quilt.
- Chart a cross-stitch label design that includes the information you wish and stitch it in colors that complement the quilt. Stitch the finished label to the quilt backing.

Metric Conversion Chart

Metric Conversion Chart	
Inches x 2.54 = centimeters (cm)	Yards x .9144 = meters (m)
Inches x 25.4 = millimeters (mm)	Yards x 91.44 = centimeters (cm)
Inches x .0254 = meters (m)	Centimeters x .3937 = inches (")
	Meters x 1.0936 = yards (yd)

Standard Equivalents					
$1/8$"	3.2 mm	0.32 cm	$1/8$ yard	11.43 cm	0.11 m
$1/4$"	6.35 mm	0.635 cm	$1/4$ yard	22.86 cm	0.23 m
$3/8$"	9.5 mm	0.95 cm	$3/8$ yard	34.29 cm	0.34 m
$1/2$"	12.7 mm	1.27 cm	$1/2$ yard	45.72 cm	0.46 m
$5/8$"	15.9 mm	1.59 cm	$5/8$ yard	57.15 cm	0.57 m
$3/4$"	19.1 mm	1.91 cm	$3/4$ yard	68.58 cm	0.69 m
$7/8$"	22.2 mm	2.22 cm	$7/8$ yard	80 cm	0.8 m
1"	25.4 mm	2.54 cm	1 yard	91.44 cm	0.91 m